Unleashing Your Brilliance

Tools & Techniques to Achieve
Personal, Professional & Academic Success

Brian E. Walsh PhD

Cover graphics © 2005 JupiterImages Corporation.

Crossword puzzles created with Eclipse Crossword - www.eclipsecrossword.com

Power Coaching®, Mind-Kinetics® and PCMK™ are registered trademarks and trademarks of Coaching and Leadership International Inc.,(CLI).

Brain Gym® is a registered trademark of the Educational Kinesiology Foundation.

PhotoReading™ is a worldwide trademark of Learning Strategies Corporation.

Time Line Therapy® training and Time Line Therapy™ techniques are registered by Dr. Tad James.

Mind Mapping™ is a trademark of Tony Buzan.

HeartMath® and Freeze-Frame® are registered trademarks of Institute of HeartMath.

TestEdge® is a registered trademark of HeartMath LLC.

DiSC® is a registered trademark of Inscape Publishing Inc.

The Holosync Solution® and Holosync® are registered trademarks of Centerpointe Research Institute

Library and Archives Canada Cataloguing in Publication

Walsh, Brian Everard, 1947—

Unleashing your brilliance: tools & techniques to achieve personal, professional & academic success / Brian E. Walsh. — 1st ed.

Includes bibliographical references and index.
ISBN 0–9738415–1–6

1. Learning, Psychology of. 2. Success—Psychological aspects.
I. Title.

BF318.W36 2005   153.1'5   C2005–903716–4

Also available in electronic version (e-book)

Walsh Seminars Ltd.
Box 963, Victoria BC V8W 2R9 Canada

www.UnleashingBook.com

Printed in Canada

This work is dedicated to my family.

Noel Justin Walsh
**Dad encouraged and directed me
in a million ways.**

Katherine Muriel (McCaul) Walsh
**Mum taught me what
unconditional love is all about.
She's also my best friend.**

Tony, Robin, Chris, Greg, and Derek.
**To my brothers and their families.
Thanks for always being
there for me.**

ACKNOWLEDGEMENTS

For their substantial contributions, I am truly indebted to the following friends and colleagues. Alex Docker, Amber Freer, Bob Proctor, Edward Butterworth, Endre Dolhai, Carol Scott, Kathryn Graham, Lance Gilson, Mavis Andrews, Paul Scheele, Ron Willard, Roxanne Rees, Sarala Godine.

For her consistant dedication to this project, I wish to thank my senior graphic designer, Kelly Hewkin, of Intuitive Graphic Design. www.intuitivegraphicdesign.com

To the many friends who proofread and edited sections of the manuscript, brainstormed titles, and contributed in many other ways, I wish to thank:

Alex Tardecilla	Georgia Foster	Linda Schaumleffel
Andre Janisch	Gillian Grigor	Lorrie Carlson
Ann Moxley	Giselle Leduc	Malcolm Ives
Anne Dickinson	Gizelle River	Marjorie Moulton
Astrid Whiting	Grace Gerry	Marlena Field
Barbara Green	Holly Chui	Matthew Ashdown
Betska K–Burr	Hugh Noble	Michael Bieber
Bruce Elkin	Jane Mackay	Michael Finer
Christine Rawlinson	Jean Phillipe De Lasalle	Michael Losier
Christopher Arbique	John Berry	Owen Rose
Craig Walsh	John Burr	Renee Deakin
Dai Davis	Julie Brown	Robin Gillmor
Dave Hallett	Karen Davis	Roy Streit
Douglas Markowitz	Karen Hallett	Ruby Walmsley
Elisa Lai	Kim Patton	Suzanne Thibodeau
Faith Shannon	Kimberly Barthel	Susan P. Smith
Fred Gordon	Lila Dahl	Thomas Dawson
	Lily Li	Willo Walker
		Yvette Eastman

Apologies to anyone whom I have missed.

Contents

TABLES

FIGURES

FOREWORD BY BOB PROCTOR

Knowledge is the observation of a fact.
Knowing is the inward experience of that fact.
Vernon Howard

If you happen to fall into the same category as I, you have very likely been conditioned to believe that you were learning when you were, in fact, merely gathering information.

Learning is when we consciously entertain an idea, let ourselves get emotionally involved in that idea, step out and act on the idea, and the action changes a result in our life. It is the feedback that we consciously receive from the change in results that is the learning experience.

This book that you hold in your hands could, very easily, turn into a treasure. I say could because you must choose to use it, study it and apply it. No amount of reading or memorizing will make you successful in life; it is the understanding and application of wise thoughts that count.

This book is truly about learning. Studying and applying the information will be a very pleasurable learning experience. The information it contains is meant for anyone who has suffered anxiety from studying for an exam or test, questioned his or her intelligence, felt out of tune with mainstream education, or simply wanted to learn more efficiently. In essence, this book is for everyone! It explains how the brain actually learns, and what you can do to take advantage of your natural learning processes.

For people fully engaged in life, whatever their age or profession, learning plays a central role, and it only makes sense that they would want to learn in the most effective way. Traditionally, school has not taught us how to learn; it's almost paradoxical!

Building on his knowledge of hypnotherapy, the unity of mind and body, and the role of emotions, Brian Walsh has captured the essence of brain-compatible learning. In easy-to-understand language, he clearly explains how our conditioning or paradigms shape habits that help or hinder learning. You need only read the introduction to appreciate the quality and value of what you'll find here.

Offering great benefits for university and corporate learners, this book will also help teachers and trainers who will discover a host of effective facilitation techniques. Although Dr. Walsh mildly admonishes outdated school methods, he has high praise for those teachers who go out of their way to accommodate the assortment of learning styles found in any classroom. In an unusual approach, each chapter ends with an interesting opportunity for you to further stimulate your brain and reinforce your absorption of the chapter's contents.

I highly recommend you use this book as a guide to making the most of your natural talent for learning in such a clear, innovative, and entertaining way.

Bob Proctor
Author of best-selling book *You Were Born Rich*
www.bobproctor.com

Brian Walsh, an international speaker based in western Canada, holds a commerce degree and a PhD in Clinical Hypnotherapy.

His dissertation was *The Efficacy of Accelerated Learning Techniques in Teaching English as a Second Language.* In addition to being a hypnotherapist, he is also an Acupuncture Detoxification Specialist, an Emotional Freedom Technique Practitioner, and a Master Practitioner of Neurolinguistic Programming.

During most of Brian's thirty-year career in the corporate world, he was responsible for human resources and training. His final appointment was as general manager for his company's China operation in Beijing. He has also lived in Canada's arctic, where he studied anthropology and served as a Justice of the Peace.

This is Brian's first book.

PREFACE

Albert Einstein called our normal state the "optical delusion of consciousness." Almost all of our awareness is processed in our conscious minds. The interesting thing is that 90 percent of our mental processing is not conscious at all. Like an iceberg, only about 10 percent is obvious.

Your brain learns in a way entirely foreign to how you have been taught. That's a bold statement, and I am asking you to suspend your beliefs in traditional learning and teaching methods while you read this book. This will be to your advantage.

My purpose in writing this book is to share what I have learned from my experience as a corporate trainer working with various cultures, and my training and research as a hypnotherapist and a practitioner of Neurolinguistic Programming. A great deal of my study dealt with what lies beyond conscious learning.

In this book you will learn how the brain processes information, and how emotions and beliefs affect learning. You will discover that the way your brain is wired can be altered both intentionally and unintentionally. With this knowledge, you can effectively apply the accelerated learning tools and techniques found in the latter part of this book.

No matter how well you think you learn, after reading this book, you will be able to achieve more, in less time, with less effort.

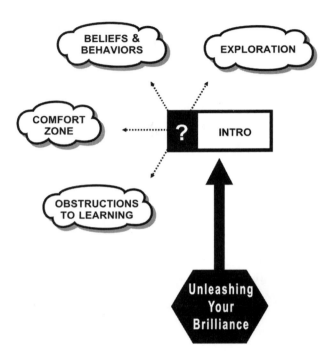

INTRODUCTION –
LET'S SET THE STAGE...

My aim in this introduction is to prepare you for what you will discover in the rest of the book. I want you to get a handle on how and why people behave as they do. I want you to see where ineffective habits come from. I want you to be aware of some of the things in life that may hinder your ability to learn.

Optimizing Your Exploration of This Book

1. Set your intention. In other words, state your purpose for reading this book and what you expect to get out of it. Write it on a large piece of paper and stick it on your wall. You may even have a few objectives (better grades, greater comprehension, personal growth, whatever). Chapter 3 contains a section on goal-setting.

> *The most important thing in life is to have a focus and a purpose*
>
> Emperor Marcus Aurelius

2. Read the table of contents twice.

3. Read the index. Use a highlighter to call attention to any entries with multiple references. They just might be important. That simple highlighter may be one of your most valuable tools. Use it often.

4.   Take a short break. Drink water. Later, I'll explain the negative effects of dehydration on thinking.

5.   Read your intention(s) out loud if you can. Do this periodically as you advance through the book.

6.   Scan the whole text, pausing at each title and subtitle.

7.   Read the table of contents and index one more time.

8.   Take a break. Drink water. This is so very important.

9.   Read this book in roughly twenty to thirty minute spurts. About every seven to ten minutes, look at a distant object for a few moments. I'll explain the advantages later. Some items are intended for trainers and teachers; however, they could be of use to anyone.

10. Each chapter ends with a review in the form of a crossword puzzle. Although you could complete it right away, I suggest that you let the material sink in for a few hours, or even overnight, before beginning this review. If you prefer not to mark up your book, we have provided the crossword blanks at www.UnleashingBook.com. The puzzle solutions are located in Appendix 4.

11. As well, most chapters end with a couple of questions for you to consider. You will then be invited to integrate what you've learned by means of an online resource. More about that in the next chapter.

12. Have fun. Share any Aha! moments with others. *Feel the energy.*

Read the following passage...
and then think about why you understand it.

> Aoccdrnig to a rscheearch at an Elingsh uinervtisy, it deosn't mttaer in waht oredr the ltteers in a wrod are, the olny iprmoetnt tihng is taht frist and lsat ltteer is at the rghit pclae. The rset can be a toatl mses and you can sitll raed it wouthit porbelm. Tihs is bcuseae we do not raed ervey lteter by itslef but the wrod as a wlohe.

Your brain is more highly developed than you may realize.

Now, don't get too smug. Examine this next passage...
and count the number of times the letter "F" occurs.

FINISHED FILES ARE THE RE–
SULT OF YEARS OF SCIENTI–
FIC STUDY COMBINED WITH THE
EXPERIENCE OF MANY YEARS.

Did you find three? Most people do.
Look for more, then see appendix 4 for an explanation.

How Core Beliefs Become Behaviors

The fences are not around the farm.
They're up here, in your heads.

Ginger... from the movie *Chicken Run*

As you explore this book you will discover things that your parents, teachers, and even neuroscientists didn't know just a decade ago. For instance, ninety-five percent of your behavior is a result of patterns and habits, most of which you acquired when you were very young. Most of us grew up with ineffective study habits. Why? Because our educators and caregivers didn't know any better. Those thousands of wasted hours sitting in classrooms and studying at home have often yielded frustration, self-limiting beliefs, and low self-esteem. Don't take it anymore! No matter what your age, you can learn with success and delight.

Freud popularized the concept of the subconscious, sometimes called the *unconscious* or the *non-conscious*. I'll use all of these words interchangeably. As you progress through this book you'll discover that, although your conscious mind has an important role to play, **learning has a great deal more to do with subconscious processing than conscious thought**. The chief responsibility of the mind is to protect; in fact, to survive. Remember this as you learn how to nourish and develop your mind.

Let me use an analogy to explain the power of the subconscious mind. If your feet are flat on the floor, the area under your feet corresponds to the processing ability of your conscious mind. The floor area in the room not covered by your feet represents the power of your subconscious mind. Your conscious mind operates at about 126 bits per second, while your subconscious mind is 10,000 times faster than that. As you can see, **the power is really in the subconscious**. That is the common thread you will find in this book.

Elephant trainers use a very interesting technique to harness their animals. When the elephant is still very young, the trainers attach one end of a strong chain to one of the elephant's legs, and the other end to a stake firmly driven into the ground. This allows the animal the freedom of a very defined circle. While harnessed day after day, the elephant **learns** that this circle is its only territory. As the years go by, the chain is exchanged for thinner and thinner ropes. The trainers know that the elephant could walk away at any time, but the elephant doesn't catch on, and so remains within the defined circle.

What's your circle? What are your self-limiting beliefs?

Let me tell you a short story about a newly-wed couple. It was their first thanksgiving dinner together and the new "Mrs." wanted to show off her culinary skills. When the turkey was brought to the table, the hubby asked, "Why is the end of the turkey cut off?" She said that this was the way to cook a turkey. Asked where she got that idea, she answered that her mother always cooked it that way. When her mother was asked to explain this method, she simply said that her mother always did it that way. When the grandmother was asked why she cut the end of the turkey, she simply said, "My pan was too small." (See section on Beliefs in Chapter 9.)

Now, here is a last thought about beliefs. How often have you heard someone rationalize incomplete action by saying, "**Well, I tried**"? To **try** is a cop-out. It's an escape hatch. **Try** is one word that I would like you to remove from your vocabulary, unless you are talking about legal trials. When we promise to do something by saying that we'll try, we're setting ourselves up for failure. Listen to news reports or the speeches of politicians. They are rife with that word. Be prepared to put your reputation on the line. Instead of using that word, say "**I'll do my best...**" Can you feel the difference?

Do or do not; there is no try.

Yoda to Luke in *Star Wars*

You cannot try to do things.
You simply must do things.

Ray Bradbury
Author of *The Martian Chronicles*
and *Fahrenheit 451*

We are continually faced with great opportunities...
which are brilliantly disguised as unsolvable problems.

Margaret Mead

A ship in the harbor is safe, but that's not what ships are made for.

Unknown

Your Comfort Zone

As infants, we learned hundreds of times faster than we do as adults. Why? Because everything was novel and exciting. We learned at our own pace and we blossomed. Humans seek out and thrive on predictability. Most people have a tendency to seek out "their" magazines, music, movies, and TV shows. This only makes sense; adults create comfort zones of predictability.

If we linger in our own comfort zone, we are intentionally limiting our exposure to new material. If you want to grow, if you want to excel, if you want to become all you can be — then move to the edge of the zone. This is known as the *area of chaos*. This is where learning takes place. It may be uncomfortable for a short while, and the payoff is worth it.

One must still have chaos in
oneself to be able to give birth to a
dancing star.

Friedrich Wilheim Nietzsche

Don't be afraid to go out on a limb.
That's where the fruit is.

H. Jackson Browne

In Stephen Covey's *The 7 Habits of Highly Effective People*, the seventh habit is "Sharpen the Saw." This means taking time out for self-improvement. By reading this book, you are demonstrating that you are undeniably committed to your personal growth. For that, you deserve to be congratulated.

Anyone who stops learning is old,
whether twenty or eighty.
Anyone who keeps learning today
is young.

The greatest thing in life is to
keep your mind young.

Henry Ford

Be Aware of Obstructions to Your Learning

Let's spend a bit of time identifying things in your life that may hinder your progress. What follows are many of the sources of poor memory and learning. These work against your best interests.[1]

- **Environmental factors** such as classroom or office light, temperature, air, cleanliness, acoustics, and teaching aids (whiteboards, projectors) have a great influence on learning. Remember when classrooms were set up so that the windows were on the students' left? That was great… if you happened to be right-handed.

  A study of European schools located near airports found a significant negative impact of aircraft noise on children's reading, cognition, and memory[2]. Stress from chronically noisy environments can lead to increased feelings of helplessness. When a Munich airport was shut down, the deficit disappeared.[3] A similar study in Montreal confirmed these findings.[4] Curiously, constant noise from vehicular traffic has no measurable negative consequences.

- **Rigid school systems** work against many learners. The low-level skill testing, developmentally-inappropriate curricula and the disregard for individual learning styles have a demoralizing effect on learners.

> *The authority of those who teach is very often a hindrance to those who wish to learn.*
>
> Cicero

(See *Learning Styles* in Chapter 7.) Do you have any idea if you take in information more easily by seeing, hearing, or touching?

- **Competition** in home, school, work, and social environments causes stress because of inappropriate expectations. Social conformity, competition in sports, and generally living in a win/lose world contributes to lower self-worth.

- **Nutritional deficits** point to inadequate amounts of proteins, lack of amino acids and fatty acids, as well as to diets high in simple carbohydrates, like sugar and white flour products. According to *Behavior, Learning & Health*, a new booklet being released by the nonprofit Feingold Association of the United States (FAUS), certain synthetic food additives and foods can trigger symptoms of hyperactivity, attention deficits, and other health problems in chemically sensitive children and adults.[5] Many school districts, having lost much of their government financial support, have allowed commercial fast-food vending machines in schools as fund-raising ventures. Some parent and teacher groups are instigating reconsideration of these shortsighted decisions. One example is the Central Alternative School in Appleton, Wisconsin, where they were experiencing excessive behavioral difficulties with the students. In 1997, vending machines were replaced, and the cafeteria began to serve wholesome food. Episodes of suicide, drop-out, and weapons violations dropped to virtually zero. This book's website www.UnleashingBook.com has a link to the Feingold Association site. Please see appendix 3 for a list of symptoms resulting from poor nutrition.

> *Not taking care of your body is like*
> *not paying your rent;*
> *you end up with no place to live.*
>
> Author and world marathon record holder,
> the late Dr. Gayle Olinekova

- **TV, computers and video games**. Although each of these has positive educational and developmental aspects, they also increase exposure to violence, decrease imaginative stimulation, minimize interpersonal interaction (resulting in poor social skills), and cause ocular lock (staring).

- **Developmental problems** follow a lack of sensory stimulation, lack of movement, lack of touch, lack of interactive creative play and communication. Some of these symptoms are common in *Attachment Disorder*. (See Chapter 8.)

- **Neurological Disorganization.** Misalignments caused by a childhood fall can go undetected, causing problems in the flow of energy throughout the body. Such a child will essentially be running on less power, and aside from a number of physical ailments, may also have behavioral and school problems with listening, speaking, reading, writing, concentration, problem-solving, and memorizing.

- **Electrical challenges** result from inadequate water consumption, lack of oxygen, and excessive exposure to electromagnetic fields (EMF). Dehydration of just 5 percent can cause up to a 30 percent decrease of mental capacity. Many people are unaware of the diuretic effects of many of the liquids they consume, such as coffee and alcohol.

- **Medical problems** begin in the womb. *Fetal Alcohol Syndrome* (FAS) is a cluster of birth defects caused by a mother's consumptions of alcohol during pregnancy. It is typified by low birth weight and decreased mental functioning. Stress experienced by the expectant mother will also impact the fetus. Conditions that can contribute to learning difficulties in children are infections, allergies, yeast overgrowth, improper medications, inadequate diet or sleep, substance abuse, child abuse, poor vision, and poor hearing.

> *To keep the body in good health is a duty ...*
> *otherwise we shall not be able to keep our minds strong and clear.*
>
> Buddha

- **Time wasters** are often so subtle that we treat them as "the way things are." They include: lack of objectives or priorities, shuffling paperwork, constant interruptions, indecision, switching priorities, personal disorganization, cluttered desk or work area, attempting too much, being unable to say "no," limited access to required equipment or materials, leaving tasks unfinished, inadequate/inaccurate/delayed information, unnecessary socializing, plunging into a task without planning, lack of self-discipline, and exhaustion.

Now that we have laid the groundwork, I want to introduce you to two tools in the next chapter. These will help you with the absorption of the material in this book.

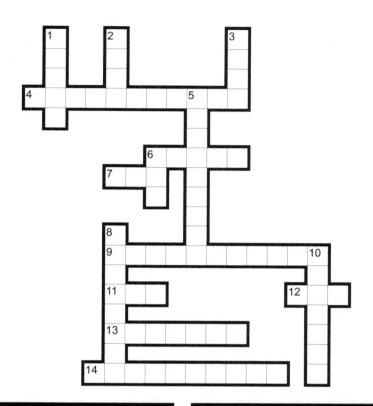

ACROSS

4. A "win–lose" obstruction
6. Popularized the concept of the subconscious
7. An insightful moment
9. Other word for subconscious
11. Yoda, "there is no _____"
12. "sharpen the _____"
13. Primary directive of the mind
14. Low on water

DOWN

1. Area on the edge of the comfort zone
2. A ship in the harbor is _____
3. A quick preview of the whole book
5. What you expect to get form this book
6. Result of alcohol during pregnancy
8. Entries with _____ references in index might be important
10. Ocular lock

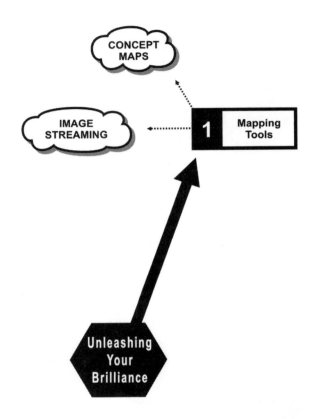

1

NAVIGATE WITH THESE MAPPING TOOLS

> *The Mind Map is an expression of radiant thinking and is therefore a natural function of the human mind.*
>
> *It is a powerful graphic technique which provides a universal key to unlocking the potential of the brain*
>
> Tony Buzan,
> developer of Mind Mapping™6

More than any other sense, visual processing involves almost 80 percent of your brain. Research has shown that images can improve memory three times better than repetition.[7] I want you to get as much value from this book as possible, so I am introducing two tools that you can use as you read each chapter.

Concept Maps

Memory is naturally associative, not linear. Associative means finding relationships between new and existing information, thereby creating links. Accelerated learning guru Eric Jensen says that some types of memory are "activated by association, similarities, or contrasts."

The disadvantages of taking traditional linear notes include writing down unessential words, which wastes time and energy. Other information may be missed while noting down one idea. Associations and connections between key words and ideas are not readily apparent, attention wanders easily, and the lack of color and other visual qualities handicaps memory. Since the notes are linear in form, they are laborious to review. Tony Buzan, quoted above, estimates that Mind Mapping™ eliminates over 90 percent of unnecessary words in note taking.

The concept map is a management and personal development tool that utilizes both sides of the brain. Originally designed as a method for taking notes, it can be used for planning, organizing thoughts, and problem solving. Concept maps are also known as pictograms, graphic organizers, thinking maps, activity maps, mind maps, and idea maps.

Concept maps use only key words and significant images, allowing a great deal more information to be placed on a single page. They can provide a bird's eye view and, because they are graphic, the learner's attention is crystallized. This is known as the *picture superiority effect* (better memory for pictures than words). The *picture* referred to here is not necessarily just images, but also the structural links. Mapping engages much more of the brain in the process of assimilating, evaluating, and connecting facts than does conventional note taking. It consolidates information from different sources, prompts new ideas, and assists thinking through complex problems. Since it is on a single sheet of paper, it is more compact than conventional notes, allowing quick review. Once the map is drawn, additional information can be easily integrated with little disruption.

You will notice a small map of each chapter as you progress through this book.

Creating the Map

An idea has thousands of links in the mind. Mapping enables these links and associations to be recorded and reinforced. Starting from the center of an unlined page, a map encourages expansion in all directions. The main topic lines radiate in all directions from the center. It is also possible to have two starting points. Sub-topics and facts will branch off these lines like branches and twigs from the trunk of a tree. The structure produced will evolve of its own accord.

Creativity bolsters memory. Employing some of the best practices in creating a map will yield a superior design. Here are some tips:

- Use single, meaningful nouns and verbs as keywords on the connecting lines. This reinforces the structure and co-herence of the notes.

- Print rather than writing in script to make it more read-able and memorable.

- Use lower case since it is more visually distinctive and better remembered than upper case.

- Use color to depict themes and associations to make items stand out.

- Think in three-dimension and employ arrows, symbols, and other visual aids to show links between different ele-ments.

- To maintain creativity, brainstorm continually. Don't

judge or hold back; move around the map and don't get stuck in one area.

- Jot down ideas as they occur, wherever they fit. Some people begin by putting ideas on sticky-notes.

- Here is a novel approach: If you run out of ideas, record your voice listing the elements in the map. Then play it back as you look at the map. New links and ideas often bubble up.

- If you run out of space, paste more paper onto the map. Break boundaries and think outside the box. As new information surfaces, link it into the map appropriately. Flip-chart paper is great for these maps. Newspapers often sell newsprint roll-ends at a reasonable cost.

Here is a suggestion: Create a map of this book **before** you read it. This will prepare your mind for all the information it will be receiving. How do you do that? Simply build the map from the table of contents. Use poster-sized paper. As you advance through the book, you can add insights and links.

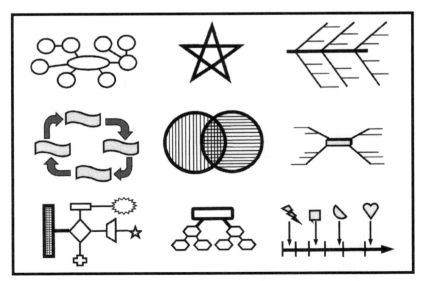

Figure 1.1 Samples of Various Concept Maps

Image Streaming

A child's active imagination begins to atrophy as adulthood approaches. As we mature, the day-to-day world in which we live demands greater left-brain thinking. Great minds such as Albert Einstein and Leonardo da Vinci were bilateral thinkers. This means that they were able to take advantage of more brainpower.

Einstein was a master at image-streaming. He would "turn off" his logical left brain and "turn on" his resourceful right brain. This allowed ideas and solutions to flow for whatever issue or question he was dealing with. The right brain "flow" would come in the form of images, as well as muscular sensations and feelings. Einstein became a master at using his left brain to decode these images into innovative solutions for his challenge. With training and practice in image-streaming, all of us can become greater whole-brain learners.

I invite you to get as much value from this book as possible. To help you assimilate the information, I will ask a couple of questions at the end of most chapters. You will then have the option to access some internet resources. One is called The Brain Walk®. Since there is more than one version of The Brain Walk®, you will be advised which to use after each chapter. These online tools have been designed, and provided at no cost to you, by Coaching and Leadership International Inc.

When you do The Brain Walk®, not only will you gain new insights into what you have already read, but also your brain will actually be preparing for material you haven't yet covered.

But wait – There's more! All of this activity will be encouraging your brain hemispheres to communicate with each other. This means that you will become a more whole-brain thinker.

The benefits of using these tools at the end of a chapter and every day for the rest of your life include:

- Your right brain will "pull an Einstein" and provide you with quick innovative solutions to your daily challenges. Once you get good at it, The Brain Walk® will take you just two to three minutes per day.

- You will more easily eliminate your negative self-talk that thwarts progress towards greater success.

- You will more easily eliminate your blaming and judging thoughts of others. Just think about it! Freedom comes when these people cannot steal our power anymore. And there have been many reported cases of people actually liking each other!

- This tool of genius creates bilateral thinkers. With constant use, you will notice an improvement in your ability to switch easily between left and right hemispheres, meaning faster thought processing. Awesome.

- You will notice improvements in focus and productivity.

- We all seek answers to life. The Brain Walk® will give you the clarity you need every day to tap into your highest creative centers for answers.

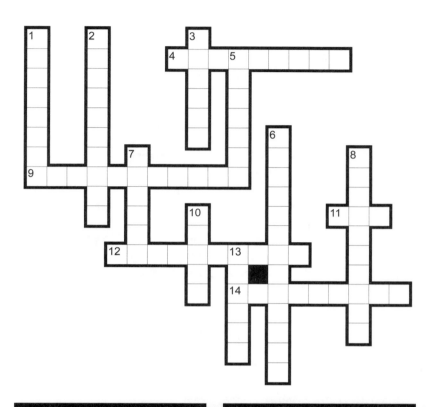

ACROSS

4. Einstein and da Vinci, were _____ thinkers
9. Picture _____ effect
11. Mind Maps use just _____ words
12. _____ bolsters memory
14. Einstein was a master at image–_____

DOWN

1. Sub-topics and facts are like tree _____
2. They sell off roll-ends
3. Mind Maps have more information on a _____ page

DOWN

5. As adulthood approaches, a child's active imagination begins to _____
6. Not judging or holding back is part of this
7. Memory is not _____
8. Imagery improved memory three times better than _____
10. Mind Maps were originally for taking _____
13. About 80% of the brain is involved in _____ processing

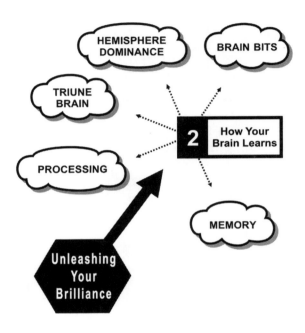

HOW YOUR BRAIN LEARNS

The brain is made to be challenged

Dr. Jerre Levy,
University of Chicago

There is a treasure chest of gems hidden in the following pages. When you find them, they will enhance and brighten your understanding of the whole book.

Plato described the brain as being like a ball of wax that becomes grooved during the learning process, and said that recalling information is accomplished by "reviewing" these grooves. Aristotle thought that the heart was the source of memory, and that the brain simply cooled the blood. In the seventeenth century, Descartes suggested that fluids in the brain controlled motor activity, and that mental processing existed in the mind, outside of the physical brain. Around 1850, Franz Joseph Gall felt the lumps and bumps on people's heads in an attempt to discover people's predispositions.

The brain is the only organ in the body that sculpts itself from outside experience. In a sense, your experience becomes biology. Until quite recently, methods of observing the cognitive activity and organization of the brain were relatively limited in scope and value. Scientists derived their data by means of intrusive experiments on animals and the study of autopsied brains of people who had various cognitive and/or motor impairments. The processes were not only difficult; they were principally inferential and open to misinterpretations. Only in the last decade have technological advances allowed real-time observation of the process of learning in a live human brain. As of 2005, about 99 percent of what was known about how the human brain learns had been revealed in just the previous six years.

Recent progress in computerized imaging technology has made it possible to technologically observe, amplify, record, rapidly analyze, and graphically display substances and signals that reflect activity in very specific brain regions.

Functional Magnetic Resonance Imaging (fMRI) measures brain blood flow patterns and metabolic changes. It can detect specific brain regions that are active when the subject is carrying out a task such as reading, making a decision, or moving a specific muscle. This technology can identify differences of the brain anatomy and activity for people who read well versus those who read poorly, or for those who make appropriate versus inappropriate decisions.

Positron Emission Tomography (PET) employs a small amount of radioactively-tagged glucose (or other compound) introduced into the bloodstream of the experimental subject. Since glucose is the brain's principal food, the PET scans of subjects reveal activity areas of the brain during specific cognitive or physical activities.

PET uses radioactive isotopes, and fMRI uses powerful magnets; therefore their use in educational research is limited by both ethical and financial considerations. The best potential for educational researchers is found in electroencephalogram (EEG) technology. It is the least invasive, least expensive, and most portable of the imaging technologies. It measures electrical brain waves via electrodes placed on the skull. Researchers eventually may be able to observe brain activity in non-laboratory settings, such as a classroom.

Brain Bits

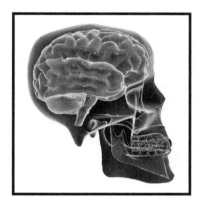

Many functions of the brain (language, music, vision, thought and socialization) are highly localized. Learning specific tasks appears to alter unique and distinct regions of the brain. Brain reorganization has been verified in the language functions of deaf individuals, in rehabilitated stroke patients, and in the visual cortex of people who are blind from birth. (See Chapter 4 on *Intelligences* for locations of specific traits.)

Neuroscientists tell us that the brain has a great number of specialized modules that are developed under genetic control. Symptoms of brain-damaged patients include loss of speech, or the inability to understand spoken or written language (*aphasias*). These symptoms differ, depending on which part of the brain has been injured. The neural connections that have been lost in disorders like stroke need to be re-mapped, and this may be possible through a combination of learning and drug therapy.

One of the brain's most remarkable traits is its *plasticity* – its ability to reorganize neural pathways by experience. Learning and memory employ this capability, as does the brain's ability to recover after some forms of injury. Observations using fMRI have shown that areas of the brain can reorganize to take over the tasks previously carried out by damaged regions. Also, new areas can be recruited, but only within well-defined processing systems.

There appear to be separate brain areas that specialize in subtasks such as hearing words (spoken language of others), seeing words (reading), speaking words (speech), and generating words (thinking with language). The left hemisphere of the brain is the seat of language facility. Injury in the left frontal lobe results in subjects understanding well, but their speech is slow, labored, and poorly articulated; damage to the left temporal lobe results in a flood of nonsensical speech. *Anomic aphasics* have word-finding deficits. *Conduction aphasics*, while having fluent meaningful speech, produce many errors in pronunciation. Other examples of aphasics are patients who can speak but not read, read but not write, write but not read (even what they've just written), and other combinations. Speech and comprehension are clearly located in different parts of the brain. There is also an affliction known as *deep dyslexia*. In this case, the deep dyslexic may read the word "apple," and unknowingly say a related item, such as "fruit" or "flower."

A Brief Look at Hemispheric Differences

Some of the earlier-mentioned non-invasive imaging technologies can measure electrical activity and blood-flow velocity in the brain's left and right mid-cerebral arteries. Discrete activities reveal considerable differentiation even in slightly different tasks. For example, in one experiment, subjects were asked to focus on **what** was said (semantics). Blood flow velocity went up in the left side of the brain. When they shifted attention to **how** it was said (tone of voice, whether happy, sad, angry, afraid or neutral) blood flow also went up in the right side, but didn't reduce in the left side. It seems that the left side processes the semantic meaning of words automatically, even if we focus on the tone. The left side stays active to label the emotion.[8]

A 2003 study by the Wellcome Trust of Britain found that, unlike English speakers whose left-brain is active when listening or speaking, Mandarin Chinese speakers use both sides of their brains to understand language. The researchers proposed that since Mandarin is a highly tonal language, the tones account for this right-side activity.[9] I suggest that the right-side activity is due to the fact that the right hemisphere handles graphics and symbols. The written form of Chinese is ideographic (written symbol representing an idea or object.) This would probably apply to the many other Asian languages that are ideographic. Educators working with children with learning challenges in Philadelphia found that they could teach them to read Chinese characters more easily than the English alphabet.[10] This finding reflects the strong right-brained spatial intelligence of children. (See Chapter 2 on *Hemispheric Dominance* and Chapter 4 on *Intelligence*.)

Learning and the Brain

Although the brain accounts for only 2 percent of our body weight, it uses over 20 percent of all the oxygen, 25 percent of all blood flow, over 30 percent of the water the body takes in, and 40 percent of all the nutrients consumed. If the brain is dehydrated by just 5 percent, the neurotransmitter activity is reduced by 30 percent. This results in fuzzy thinking, fatigue, stymied decision-making, impaired short-term memory, and diminished focus and concentration. Sensible nutritional habits are vital in keeping the brain fueled with the energy required to operate at its optimum capacity.

Neurocognitive research has provided evidence that both the developing and the mature brain are structurally altered during learning. This *brain plasticity* means that learning changes the physical structure and functional organization of the brain. In other words, practice and experience trigger plasticity. Under some conditions, both the cells that provide support to the neurons and the capillaries that supply blood to the nerve cells may be altered as well. It's not the number of brain cells that determines a person's ability to achieve and succeed; when we learn something new, *dendrite spiny protuberances* start to grow out of the dendrite spines of our neurons. As we learn, they advance toward each other and create links. The amount of these dendrite spiny protuberances we grow in our brain determines our abilities, intelligence, and success levels. We aren't born with them; they grow during our entire lifetime as we learn. Different parts of the brain may be ready to learn at different times. Alterations in the brain that occur during learning seem to make the nerve cells more efficient or powerful.

In 1990, the US National Institute of Health asked 1500 neurosurgeons if they believed that brain cells are able to rebuild themselves (*neurogenesis*) after having been destroyed by surgery or trauma. Ninety-five percent of these neurosurgeons believed that this was not possible. In 1998, a joint Swedish-American neuro-scientific team announced that in the brain of adult humans, new brain cells could indeed regenerate. This growth of replacement cells is encouraging for those who would otherwise despair as a result of losing faculties through stroke or other brain damage. Mental decline in older people is commonly thought to be the result of dying brain cells. In fact, brain cells atrophy just like physical muscles when not exercised regularly. As with many things in life… **Use it or lose it.**

Neuroscience is the study of molecular biology, anatomy, chemistry, and physiology of the nervous system. Specifically, it explores sensation and perception, brain development – with particular interest in how brain activity relates to behavior, learning, and memory. It also studies movement, sleep, stress, aging, and neurological and psychiatric disorders. The convergence of its evidence with that of educational psychology and cognitive psychology has brought us to where we are today.

Certain conditions contribute to the efficient learning of new tasks or concepts.[11]

- **Frequency:** The more a person performs any new skill, the stronger the neural pathways become. Repeated performance enhances proficiency.

- **Intensity:** Concentrated practice furnishes greater support for a skill in a shorter time frame. Honing reading skills is similar to practicing for a marathon.

- **Cross-Training:** Being given the opportunity to experience a wide range of skills or subjects reinforces a student's overall grasp of the information, while concurrently focusing on one or two specific skill sets.

- **Adaptivity:** In order to learn and progress in specific subject material, it is crucial that the learners be challenged just beyond their capability. This ensures that they remain interested, yet not frustrated.

- **Motivation and Attention:** In order to sustain and reinforce attention and motivation, it is important to design programs incorporating several motivational strategies.

  For complex learning to occur, three interactive and mutually-supportive elements are required:

- **Relaxed alertness** is an optimal state of mind, which consists of low threat and high challenge. It exists when adequate support is combined with just enough workload to stretch the capabilities of the learner.

- **Purposeful immersion** is achieved through methodically creating a rich learning environment. Instruction, hands-on activities, guest speakers, and resource material are provided in a clutter-free brain-friendly setting.

- **Active processing** is when a learner consciously understands the material, organizes it into a coherent structure, and finally integrates it with existing knowledge.

Geoffrey and Renate Caine, authors of *12 Brain/Mind Learning Principles in Action (2005)* developed these principles based on a wide range of disciplines, including cognitive psychology, sociology, philosophy, education, technology, sports psychology, creativity research, and physics:

1. All learning engages the physiology.

2. The brain/mind is social.

3. The search for meaning is innate.

4. The search for meaning occurs through patterning.

5. Emotions and patterning are inter-dependent.

6. The brain/mind processes parts and wholes simultaneously.

7. Learning involves both focused attention and peripheral perception.

8. Learning is both conscious and unconscious.

9. There are at least two approaches to memory.

10. Learning is developmental.

11. Complex learning is enhanced by challenge and inhibited by threat associated with helplessness and fatigue.

12. Each brain is uniquely organized.

Check www.UnleashingBook.com for links to the Caine Learning Institute and their books.

Brain Specialization for Social Perception

A century ago, Charles Darwin suggested that frowns, smiles, anger, and other signals of **emotional tone** were the result of evolution. Our species has developed a fine discrimination for voice and face recognition, as well as smell. This ability classifies the elements to unconsciously decode intentions such as friendliness, threat, indifference, surprise, fright, etc.

AUDITORY: When we hear a person speak, three elements are decoded simultaneously: *voice recognition* identifies the speaker, *language perception* indicates what is being said, and the *tone* uncovers the emotional affect. Three separate parts of the brain categorize each of these factors. The subconscious is constantly busy sorting, filtering, generalizing, and deleting the millions of bits of information that are received every second. What an impressive feat that a blended, indistinct acoustic input is processed as three distinct kinds of information conveying identification, and even intent!

VISUAL: The visual portion of this innate ability absorbs **emotionally-based** facial expressions, gestures, and postures, which are instantly understood cross-culturally without effort. A smile is understood universally to mean the same thing. There are, however, many visual expressions that are entirely **culturally based**. For example, to signify "no," the Inuit (Eskimo) of the arctic, crinkle their noses (to most of us it means disgust.) To indicate "yes" they raise their eyebrows (to most of us this means interest or a question.) The signal used by some westerners to indicate "slow down" *or* "quiet-down" is an arm extended in front with the hand waving up and down; the same motion means "come here" to Asians.

OLFACTORY: Unlike all the other senses, smell does not pass through the thalamus and is therefore not subjected to the analysis and filtering that the other systems undergo. Smell has a direct track to the limbic system. This may explain why smell can generate immediate, and often vivid, memories and emotions. (See Chapter 10 about *NLP.*) A recent study[12] demonstrated that pleasant and unpleasant odors elicit activity in different parts of the human brain. Subjects were exposed to three pleasant and three unpleasant odors. The fMRI indicated that the pleasant odors activated a specific section of the brain and unpleasant odors stimulated a completely different part. This study confirms that differing odors evoke strong emotional responses. A testament to that is the success of the multi-billion dollar perfume industry.

Some limited research has demonstrated that smell can aid in learning and recall. In one study, high school students in Portland, Oregon, were exposed to a floral aroma during a test, which appeared to improve their scores from 14 to 54 percent. *Aromatherapy* has been used by NASA (United States National Aeronautic and Space Administration) in the form of a boiling pot of cinnamon/apple potpourri to relax the astronauts. Although more anecdotal than scientific, the resulting reports of better moods is worthy of note. Valerie Ann Worwood's book *The Fragrant Mind (1996)* suggests that citrus smells promote mental awareness; basil is awakening; coriander enlivens and motivates; geranium is uplifting; narcissus is empowering and creative; peppermint is clarifying, awakening, stimulating, and refreshing; and thyme is empowering.[13] When properly used, lavender oil aroma can lift mood, reduce stress, and enhance sleep.[14]

So far, we have learned that the brain is a dynamic organ that becomes stronger through challenge. Let's deepen our understanding by examining how different parts of the brain interact as a team.

Whole-Brain Learning – Hemispheric Dominance

> *Each hemisphere of the human brain has its own private sensations, perceptions, thoughts and ideas, all of which are cut off from the corresponding experiences in the opposite hemisphere. In many respects, each disconnected hemisphere appears to have a separate mind of its own.*
>
> Dr. Roger Sperry,
> Nobel Prize in Medicine, 1981

Whole-brain learning or *bilateral learning* often refers to inter-hemispheric communication. The analytical left hemisphere is better with sequencing, language, details, and creating internal dialogues (interpreting events). The right hemisphere manages spatial information; it works randomly, synthesizes, and deals with wholes (the big picture). Dr. Carla Hannaford used the terms logic hemisphere and gestalt hemisphere in her book *The Dominance Factor*, because some people are reversed in their hemispheric characteristics. For simplicity, the terms *left* and *right* are being used in this book. (See Chapter 8.) These differences between the left-brain and right-brain are very clear, anatomical and functional. Every brain simultaneously perceives and creates parts and wholes and is designed to perceive and generate patterns. The power is in harnessing the power of both halves of the brain.

LEFT HEMISPHERE	RIGHT HEMISPHERE
Focus is on parts, pieces, or details	Focus is on the big picture first
Successive, sequential, linear	Simultaneous, parallel, multiple
Logical	Creative
Internal focus	External focus
Analytical	Synthetic, associative, spatial
Aggressive, enjoys leadership roles	Passive
Controls feelings	Free with feelings
Structure-oriented	People-oriented
Seeks differences	Seeks similarities
Future-oriented	Deals with the NOW or the past
Planned and Orderly; likes instructions	Impulsive, fluid, random, flow
Sense of time (punctual)	Atemporal (unpunctual)
Literal	Meaning, metaphorical
Linguistic, symbolic	Comprehensive and configuration
Verbal intelligence	Practical intelligence
Recalls people's names	Recalls people's faces
Speaks with few gestures	Gestures when speaking
While studying, prefers bright lights	While studying, prefers frequent mobility
Intellectual	Sensuousness, intuitive
Words, letters, syntax, semantics	Emotions, tones, pictures, graphs
Lyrics to a song	Tune to a song
Quantifiable knowledge	Experiential knowledge
Mathematical calculation	Apprehension of patterns

Table 2.1   Traits of Opposing Brain Hemispheres

Generally, humans possess a hemispheric dominance expressed in terms of behavior, learning style, and, to some degree, personality. Extreme examples are "right-brained" artists and "left-brained" accountants.

When you read Chapter 9, you will see a table dealing with characteristics of the subconscious and the conscious minds. You may notice some similarities.

Basic Rest-Activity Cycle

Building on the hemispheric differences is a biorhythm known as the *Ultradian Rhythms* or *Basic Rest-Activity Cycle* (BRAC). While some biological cycles last for many days, the BRAC oscillates at between 90 and 120 minutes, consistently, around the clock.

During the **active portion** (peak performance period) of the cycle, there is greater electrical activity in the **left** hemispheric, a verbal cognitive mode, and the *autonomic nervous system* (ANS) is in a mode of sympathetic predominance.[15] This means that it is "open for business." Heightened physical activity, mental alertness, and energy mean that logic, rationality, and a "black and white" approach are being exercised.

During the **rest portion** (healing response) of the cycle, there is increased right hemispheric electrical activity, a spatial cognitive mode, and a settling down of the autonomic nervous system. Midway through the rest cycle is a trough of about twenty-minutes. This is when many cells of the brain that hold critical messenger molecules, such as *adrenaline*, are nearing empty. At this point, all the cells in the body are taking time out to replenish, rejuvenate, and rebalance. It is during this part of the cycle that people daydream and can be most creative.

The following diagram shows the oscillating brain wave frequencies during a twenty-four hour period. The peaks are the active portion of the cycle, and the valleys are the rest portion. Please also check out the section on brain waves in Chapter 9.

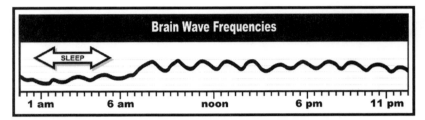

Figure 2.1   Typical BRAC Cycles During a Full Day

People who are continuously over-stimulated do not have the opportunity to recharge their internal batteries. The *central nervous system* (CNS), having to contend with the ever-constant activity, will prevent the resting period, resulting in exhaustion in the short-term, and burnout in the long-term.

To better equip a person for dealing with stress, techniques exist to maximize the resources of each side of the brain. An interesting indicator of which side is dominant at any given time is to simply breathe in through the nostrils. The nostril that draws in the greater amount of air is a contra-lateral indicator of the dominant side. In other words, if the right nostril draws more air, then the left hemisphere is dominant, indicating that the person is presently in the active part of the cycle. One technique to alter the dominance is *uni-nostril forced breathing*. In this case, to switch dominance to the right, the person would block the right nostril and force breathing in and out of the left nostril. This would be appropriate if someone wanted the right brain active for a brainstorming exercise or any creative endeavor.

A more functional endeavor, in the long-term, is to encourage whole-brain activity. Here are some techniques to enrich inter-hemispheric communication. Use your non-dominant hand to hold a cup or use a toothbrush. Experiment with your eyes closed, while navigating around your home, dressing, and even taste-testing a beverage. Drive a new route to and from work. Perform cross-lateral physical exercises and eye movement exercises. (See chapter 8.)

Whole-Brain Learning – Triune Brain

The human brain has three separate, yet dynamically interconnected, parts known as the *Triune Brain*; it incorporates the *Reptilian Brain,* the *Limbic System,* and the *Neocortex.* Through understanding their individual functions and symbiotic interactions, we can better understand accelerated learning. Research by Paul MacLean, from the United States National Institute of Mental Health illustrates that learning, retention, and behavior are powerfully influenced by human drives and needs. The somewhat different needs of the three parts of the human brain are always present and must be met continuously for effective learning.

Located in the brainstem, at the top of the spine, the reptilian brain is responsible for our survival. When we are threatened, automatic functioning, like our circulatory and respiratory systems, takes precedence over the needs of the higher levels of the brain. It is important to understand the *fight/flight/freeze* reaction, (also known as the fight-or-flight cycle), because stress in any form will tend to weaken the neocortex, thereby confusing cognitive thinking. A classic example of this is "test-taking anxiety," which causes the brain to down-shift to survival mode. On the positive side, the reptilian brain is the seat of instinctual repetitive behavior, suitable for the traditional teaching systems that employ rote learning, discipline, routine, and precedent. Unfortunately, when those systems are used for inappropriate subjects, they produce passive learners. Memorizing formulas takes the wonderment out of subjects such as science.

Also known as the *midbrain* and the *early mammalian brain*, the limbic system lies above, and surrounds, the brain stem. It is the social brain and is used in collaborative learning. It is also responsible for long-term memory. The limbic system is also where emotions reside. Emotions have a profound effect on the quality and quantity of learning. Negative feelings have a dampening effect on learning and indeed may halt it in its tracks altogether. Positive feelings, such as joy and enthusiasm, have a profoundly positive effect on the learning process. Emotions play a critical role in deciding whether to downshift to the defensive reptilian brain or up-shift to the resourceful, thinking neocortex. Emotions cannot be separated from cognition; therefore, they are important for the storage and recall of information. (See Chapter 5 on *Emotions and Learning*.) While the nonconscious mind processes about ten thousand times faster than the conscious mind, the limbic system processes ten thousand times faster than the nonconscious.[16]

The neocortex, or *thinking brain*, is essential in the uniquely human-like functions such as language, social relationships, mental focus, decision-making, problem-solving, working memory, forward planning, choosing actions, fine movement, and creativity. In a sense, the cortex is the brain's CEO. It aids the older team members in their struggle for survival.

During the learning process, the two older parts of the brain sometimes collide with the neocortex and its new ways of thinking and behaving. The resulting discomfort is known as *cognitive dissonance*. The neocortex does its best to ignore the emotional needs of the limbic system and survival pleas of the reptilian brain. It placates them by attempting to make the learner comfortable when, in fact, learning new things is inherently uncomfortable.

Accelerated learning shows us how to navigate information, rather than simply storing it. As well, we are taught how to learn, how to imagine, and how to create value and meaning for ourselves from information and experience. Accelerated learning incorporates the tools, skills, and processes needed to create a degree of comfort by providing safety, engagement, and challenge. In the next chapter, we will take a close look at accelerated learning, but first let's look at how our brain processes information.

Information Processing

Early selection theory holds that, in order for external sensory information to be processed for meaning and permanently encoded, it must first pass through conscious awareness. This means that information not selected by the conscious mind is discarded. This theory maintains that non-selected material will not be remembered.

Replacing that theory is the *late selection theory*, which contends that multiple streams of information are received and encoded by the unconscious mind before being available to the conscious mind. Consciousness is not essential for memory and learning. (See Chapter 11 on *PhotoReading*™.)

As reported in the January 2004 issue of *Psychological Science*, a study indicated that there appears to be a phenomenon associated with visual perception operating at an unconscious level.[17] Sometimes people don't have the visual experience for several seconds after they **sense** a change. The leader of the study, noted vision researcher and associate psychology and computer science professor Ron Rensink, calls this capability *mindsight*. He explains, "People do have access to this other subsystem. Vision is not just one ability; it's not just one sense." Rensink says that, aside from conscious perceptual vision, there is also an unconscious vision for action, and these two operate as very distinct subsystems. He went on to say:

In the past, people believed that if light came into your eyes, it would have to result in a picture. If it didn't result in a picture, it must mean that it can't be vision. What I'm saying is no, that first assumption is wrong. Light can come into your eyes and do other things. There are other perceptual systems and it can result in other forms of experience. It's all vision; it's just a different kind of vision. There is nothing really magical about it. It's just a different way of perceiving, so it's a different kind of experience, which I think is actually pretty cool.

So much is still unknown. Is it attitude or mental set? How is personality involved? Why are only certain people able to demonstrate this? What part of the brain is involved? Perhaps this facility of visual perception may someday be nurtured to enhance learning. (See Chapter 11 on *PhotoReading*™.)

Patterns for how information is processed begin at about the age of two. Emotionally and physically attached to the image of the mother or other primary caretaker, a child strives to become like her. If the mother is congruent in what she says, what she does, and how she reacts to the actions of the child, then the child learns that all verbal information received means exactly what was said. Unfortunately, that doesn't suitably prepare a child for the real world. At the other extreme, if a mother's possessive, ambiguous and contradictory behavior distorts the child's understanding, that child will develop resistance and begin to suppress communication. As the child becomes an adult, he or she will always be unsure if people really mean what they say. Obviously, these are extreme. Most children have the moderating effects of human interaction with people other than the mother, and most people are a blend of both these traits.

Memory

> *Memory is the treasury and*
> *guardian of all things*
>
> Cicero

If all the data received by our senses were stored in our memory, we would soon be overwhelmed. As mentioned earlier, the subconscious sorts through the input and retains only a fraction for permanent memory storage. Every second, the eyes absorb ten million bits of information, the skin takes in one million bits, and the ears receive one-hundred thousand bits. Of these millions of bits processed, only about forty bits reach the conscious mind.[18] Data that are not deleted are sorted and filtered by the subconscious, then consigned to long-term memory.

The active brain can "remember" things that actually did not happen or that are not correct. The mind makes assumptions to link events. People "remember" words that are implicit or not stated, with the same probability as explicit words. Studies with fMRI have demonstrated that the same brain areas are activated during questions and answers about both true and false events. This may explain why false memories can seem so compelling to the individual reporting the events.

Types of Memory

Remembering – storing memories in a memory bank, and recalling them – is a biological process which involves dedicated brain structures as memory banks variously specialized for different types or categories of memory function. Knowing that memories are formed in different categories, and that they move between categories, can help in developing strategies for improving memory and learning.

There are two broad categories of memory: non-conscious, and conscious. The latter includes short-term, and long-term memory.

- **Non-conscious memory**, takes two forms. One of these, *implicit memory*, automatically stores experience and concepts and plays a role unconsciously in affecting perception. The other form, *muscle memory*, plays a role in the mechanical execution of a series of motions, as in riding a bike or playing a musical instrument, learned through repetition over time. (See chapter 8.)

- **Short-term memory**, is the working memory. It's a place for stuff that you need to hang on to for only a short time. Maintaining information for only a few seconds, it enables you to remember a current thought, and so, for instance, take part in a conversation, keep a lecture in context as it progresses, or maintain the thread of a story or movie.

- **Long-term or permanent memory:** The memory of the events and facts that we can consciously recall and verbally describe. It includes that of words, symbols, and general knowledge about our perception of the workings of the world. Information of a personal nature, things witnessed or experienced, is better remembered when associated with emotion. (See Chapter 5.)

As discussed earlier in this chapter, the brain links information on an unconscious level. You can consciously help to maximize this effect. As you perceive new input, match it as best possible to material already in your memory, by using images, sounds, key words, and concept maps. A vital ingredient for memory is reviewing, and it is effective only when done at specific times after absorbing the information. For instance after one hour, one day, one week, and six months. (See also the *Links to Learning* in Chapter 3.)

The Emotional and Thinking Brains

This is a good juncture to explain the difference between different types of stress. Unhealthy stress is either too low or too high. Healthy stress is often just called a challenge. Frequently, the distinction is conditional on how much control we perceive that we have over the stressor. In challenging situations, the body releases chemicals such as *adrenaline* and *norepinephrine*. These enhance learning by increasing motivation, sharpening our perceptions, and even strengthening our body. On the other hand, unhealthy stress raises alarms all over the body by releasing *cortisol*, the survival hormone. In this book, I use the word stress to refer to unhealthy stress.

Neuroscientist Joseph LeDoux discovered a particular relationship and interaction between the emotional and thinking brains, and identified the neural pathways that carry information from the senses to the brain. Information entering through the eyes or ears goes first to the thalamus, which acts as a sorting area to assign different information to different parts of the brain. It compares new data with existing information and decides whether to compress, absorb, or ignore the new input. If the incoming information is emotional, the thalamus sends out two signals. With survival a priority concern, the first signal goes to the emotional brain (limbic system, specifically, the amygdala), and the second to the thinking brain (neocortex). This means that the emotional brain has the information first and, in the event of an emergency, can react before the thinking brain has even received the information and had an opportunity to consider options.

In such a case, the amygdala sends instructions to the lower reptilian brain to flood the body with stress hormones. There are more neural connections going **from** the limbic emotional center **to** the neocortex than vice versa. With continued arousal of the amygdala, it is difficult to break out of the resulting fight-or-flight cycle. So reason does not rule, and we are left hanging in the middle of a crisis.

The hippocampus helps create long-term memory by assigning data to different parts of the brain. For example, the names of natural things such as vegetation and wildlife are stored in one part of the brain, while man-made items such as cars and furniture are retained elsewhere. Likewise, the event, or what happened, and its meaning are laid down in separate parts of the brain.

Emotion drives attention which, in turn, drives memory. James McGaugh, PhD, of the University of California at Irvine, said, "We believe that the brain takes advantage of the chemicals released during stress and powerful emotions to regulate the strength of storage of the memory." In an article in *Psychology Today*,[19] Journalist Jill Neimark said, "A memory associated with emotionally charged information gets seared into the brain."

It is the management of emotions that gives learners greater command over their learning.

(See Chapter 5 on *Emotions.*)

Although the brain thrives on challenge and complexity, its primary drive is survival. It needs to survive socially, economically, emotionally, and physically. The brain is pre-wired to learn and, if optimum conditions are not present, employees may **learn to fear change** in the workplace, and students may **learn to fear subjects** like math. Overwhelming stress has a detrimental effect. Researchers have evidence that high stress experienced by a pregnant woman can distress the fetus, resulting in learning difficulties for the child later in life. Among infants and toddlers, high and chronic levels of stress can make learning more difficult, perhaps even shrinking the part of the brain associated with memory.[20]

Tips to Remembering

Imagine that I recite a list to you of thirty items. I then ask you to write them down after I finish. You would remember things that are:

- at the beginning of the list
- UnUsUaL
- repeated, repeated, repeated, repeated, repeated
- at the end of the list

The first and last items are known as *primacy* and *recency*. Every study session has them. If you study for one hour, then take a break, you get one of each. If you study for twenty-five minutes, take a short break, then study another twenty-five minutes. You get double the primacy and recency events. How great is that?

Memory is not stored in a single location in the brain. It is **deconstructed** and distributed all over the cortex. The emotional content is stored in the amygdala, visual images in the occipital lobes, memory of the source in the frontal lobes, and venue is stored in the parietal lobes. Remembering is actually an act of reconstruction.

AVOID EYESTRAIN

Blink in order to reestablish your peripheral and 3–D vision. Look away from your reading material every seven to ten minutes.

Memory Decay, or loss of remembered events, is a natural phenomenon as new experiences displace existing memories. You can easily counteract this loss of learned material through periodic review, as described in *The Four Links of Effective Learning* in the next chapter. The following graphic illustrates that review can facilitate the preservation of at least 80 percent of your learned material. Without a systematic review process, the material evaporates to a 20 percent retention level, as indicated below.

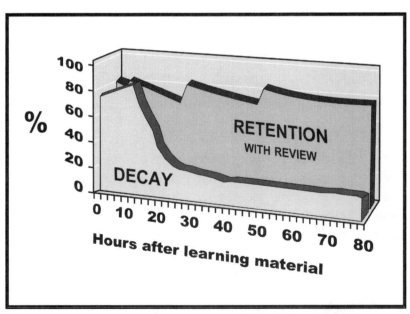

Figure 2.2   Memory Decay and Effect of Reviewing

A greater variety of input streams from eyes, ears, tactile, and emotion allow for more pathways to exist for dynamic reconstruction, thus creating richer memory. Multi-modal instruction makes a lot of sense. Accelerated Learning addresses the need.

To get a handle on just how unlimited our ability to learn is, multiply the number of neurons (10 billion) by the number of branch spines (10 million) by the number of dendrite spiny protuberances possible on each spine (100 million). The result indicates how many new connections are possible when learning. Using this size font, the answer is a "1" followed by zeros that extend for some 6.2 million miles. The capacity of our memory is virtually unlimited.

1. **What is your greatest learning from this chapter?**

2. **What is your greatest challenge with respect to how your brain is learning?**

3. **CALL TO ACTION:**
   Visit www.UnleashingBook.com to link to the CLI site. Choose to use the free self-coaching tool entitled "The Brain Walk® – A Journey for Peace of Mind". This tool will provide you with solutions to this greatest challenge.

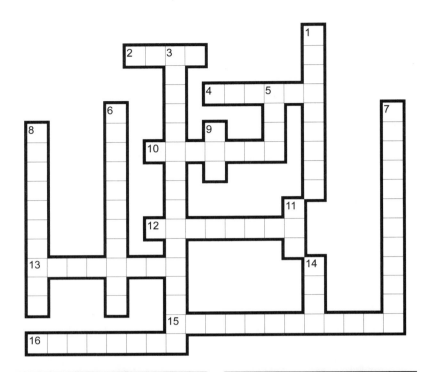

ACROSS

2. Measures brain blood flow
4. Emotional brain
10. Remembering items at end of list
12. _____ spiny protuberances
13. Muscle memory
15. 10,000 x faster than conscious
16. Smell bypasses _____

DOWN

1. Thinking brain
3. Low threat & high challenge
5. Brain is 2% of _____ weight
6. Everyday memory
7. Brain cells' ability to rebuild
8. Brain's ability to reorganize neural pathways
9. Least–invasive of imaging technology
11. Uses radioactive isotopes
14. Oscillates between 90 and 120 minutes

BRILLIANT NOTES

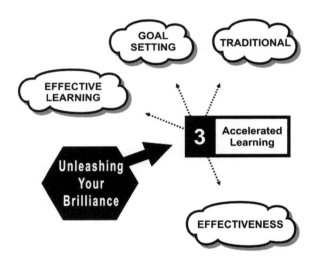

3

LET'S DISCOVER ACCELERATED LEARNING

> *Learning is the ability to acquire new knowledge or skills through instruction or experience. Memory is the process by which that knowledge is retained over time.*
>
> Authors Gerard J. Tortora
> and Sandra Grabowski (1996)

In this chapter, we'll begin by finding out the differences between accelerated and traditional methods of learning. The balance of the chapter addresses the importance of knowing where you're going, how to get there, and how to know when you've arrived.

Learners get totally involved when all their senses are stimulated through collaboration, variety, and meaningful content. Flexible methods and media accommodate all learning styles. Accelerated learning has proven to be the most advanced approach in corporate and academic instruction. **Emphasis is more on the ways the learner receives and integrates information than on the various teaching methodologies**.

Programs can be designed more quickly, measurable learning is improved, and productivity and creativity among students and employees are stimulated. Organizations are able to save time and money, which directly affects their bottom line.

Downloading information into learners' brains without them having a clear understanding of context or significance is a recipe for frustration and de-motivation. Newborns' brains are pre-programmed to perceive patterns and establish categories. They spend their infancy sorting colors, objects, shapes and concepts into sets. Social and cultural awareness is based on categorization.

The brain is not just a passive recorder of events; rather, it is actively at work both in storing and in recalling information. Learning always involves conscious and unconscious processes, blending both focused attention and peripheral perception. When a series of events is learned randomly, the mind reorders the components into sequences that make sense when recall is attempted.

The brain efficiently creates categories for processing information. In learning, memory processes create links to associated information. Learning occurs most efficiently and effectively within a structure. Experience plays an important role in building this mental structure by modifying the organization of the brain. The amount of experience in a complex environment has a direct effect on the amount of structural change. Practice increases learning.

Information's pretty thin stuff unless mixed with experience.

American writer,
Clarence Day (1874 – 1935)

Accelerated Learning is the single most important new advance in education and self–development.

Motivational speaker Brian Tracy

Accelerated Learning allows you to tap into the genius that all of us have.

Dr. Jeanette Vos,
co–author *The Learning Revolution*

Traditional versus Accelerated Learning

Below is a quick reference chart to simplify the differences between traditional learning and accelerated learning.[21]

TRADITIONAL LEARNING	ACCELERATED LEARNING
Rational, left brain	Whole brain
Mainly auditory	All sensory modalities involved
Teacher: takes responsibility for outcomes	Student: take responsibility for outcomes
Material presented at slow speed	Material presented at normal, natural speed
Teacher/curriculum centered	Student centered
Uses conscious, analytical approach	Engages subconscious processing
Not suitable for the many learners who have learning styles other than auditory and visual.	All learning styles are stimulated, therefore learning becomes fast, effective, and enjoyable

Table 3.1 Traditional Learning Versus Accelerated Learning

Traditional learning is rigid, somber and serious, compartmentalized, linear, controlling, time-based, centered on materials, and competitive. This "cookie cutter" thinking is a result of the centuries-old conviction that effective education must exist in the form of standardization, strict discipline, mind-body separation, and western scientific mechanization.

Conventional approaches to teaching are considered by some to be "brain antagonistic." They impose categories rather than encourage learners to naturally discover the appropriate categories or rules. The natural experience is to progress by a process of observation, assumption, hypothesis, generalization, trial and error, further observation, and re-evaluation of assumptions.

Unthinking respect for authority is the greatest enemy of truth.

Albert Einstein

As advantageous as the printing press was in spreading knowledge over the past five centuries, it supported linear thinking, while dampening right-brain and whole-brain processing.

Let's build on the traditional learning paradigm in which the stages of progression are:

1. Unconscious Incompetence

2. Conscious Incompetence

3. Conscious Competence

4. Unconscious Competence

Stage 1 is when you don't know how to do something, and you **don't** know that you don't know.

Stage 2 is when you **do** know that you don't know. This is where people often get stuck, discouraged by thoughts of the tough journey ahead. All of these stages may be necessary when you're learning skills requiring practice, like typing, riding a bike, or playing a musical instrument; however, when you're acquiring knowledge, accelerated learning techniques will help you speed through, or even skip stage 3.

Prior to being enrolled in formal education, children learn on many levels simultaneously because all their senses are excited and employed. Adult learning, usually standardized and mechanized, is nowhere near as efficient. Accelerated learning, however, tends to follow a more natural flow by being joyful, multi-path, inter-active, intra-active, humanistic, experiential, nurturing, multi-sensory, and results-based. People can learn simultaneously through their whole bodies and minds verbally, nonverbally, rationally, emotionally, physically, and intuitively.

Goal-Setting

An effective goal focuses primarily on results rather than activity.

Stephen R. Covey,
The 7 Habits of Highly Effective People

If you do not know where you are going, any road will take you there.

Cheshire Cat, *Alice in Wonderland*

The world always steps aside for people and organizations who know where they're going.

Miriam Larsen

It had long since come to my attention that people of accomplishment rarely sat back and let things happen to them. They went out and happened to things.

Elinor Smith

You will come across the word "goal" many times in this book. Goals are essential to your learning process because they provide direction, momentum, and motivation. Only with specific goals can you craft effective suggestions to be used in self-hypnosis. (See the section on *Self-hypnosis* in Chapter 9.)

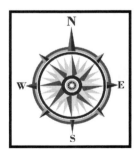

It is critical to write down your goals, since that action imprints them on your brain. Before writing your goals, identify what price you are willing to pay to achieve them. This may be material, emotional, or spiritual. At some point, expose your barriers and excuses; write them on a separate piece of paper. This list is not meant to be dwelled on; it is meant merely as acknowledgement – celebrate as you conquer each barrier or excuse.

If you are finding it difficult to decide on what you want, you could consider what author Michael Losier advised in his book, *The Law of Attraction*. He teaches a process of listing what you **don't want** as a prelude to making your definitive list of what you **do want**.

> *Once focused on the positive,*
> *you act as a magnet, to attract*
> *those things you hold in your mind.*
>
> Mark Victor Hansen co–author of
> *Chicken Soup for The Soul*

You may have heard of SMART goals. The acronym stands for *specific, measurable, attainable/agreed on, relevant,* and *timely*. My colleague Georgia Foster and I include goal-setting in our self-hypnosis workshops. We wanted to build on SMART goals, so we created the following:

- Your goal statement must always be succinctly worded in the **present tense** and in the **positive**. Use action and emotional words. Avoid negative words, future tenses, and comparisons (better, some). Let me explain why your goal statement must be positive and in the present tense. The powerhouse of accelerated learning is the subconscious mind. It is highly literal, has no concept of time, and processes in images. If you use future tenses, such as

"I will….," then the subconscious mind will not act on it since it only operates in the "NOW." Since there is no picture for a negative word (not, never, won't), then it just ignores it. If you state, "I am not attracted to chocolate cake," the subconscious only processes, "I am attracted to chocolate cake." A better wording would be, "I love foods that contribute to my body's health and vitality."

- It must be **realistic** and a **slight stretch**. Push yourself just a bit.

The greater danger for most of us
lies not in setting our aim too high
and falling short;
but in setting our aim too low,
and achieving our mark.

Michelangelo Buonarroti
(1475–1564)

- It must be **specific**, yet your assessment of your success must be **flexible**. By specific, I mean avoid comparative words. If you state, "I will be more disciplined in my work assignments," that is far too vague. To the subconscious, the word "more" may be anywhere from .0000001 percent to 100 percent more. So be specific. Celebrate each of your accomplishments, even if it is not 100 percent of what you planned. In the book, *The One-Minute Manager,* the authors counsel that if you're off course, just do a course correction – don't jump ship! Use any slip-ups as opportunities to learn.

- Your goal must be **measurable**. If you can't gauge how well you're doing, how will you know that success is actually occurring? Ensure that you pick a target date.

It must also be **paced** so that you can recognize your achievements at specific points along the way. This is the step where you take your overall goal and break it down into bite-sized modules. This chunking-down can be by subject, time, place, or resource.

- Once your mini-goals are established, **create action plans** for as many as you want. This is so important. Without an action plan, all you have is a wish-list.

> *Whatever you can do, or dream you can, begin it! Boldness has genius, magic, and power in it... Daring ideas are like chessmen moved forward; they may be beaten, but they may start a winning game.*
>
> Johann Wolfgang Von Goethe

> *Setting a goal is not the main thing.*
> *It's deciding...*
> *how you will go about achieving it,*
> *and staying with that plan.*
>
> Tom Landry, longtime coach of
> the Dallas Cowboys football team

> *Success seems to be connected with action.*
>
> Conrad Hilton,
> founder of the Hilton Hotel Chain

- **Announce** or share your goal with people who will be supportive. This emotional investment puts your reputation on the line.

- The last element is **in your face**. Write out your goals, cut out magazine pictures, or draw them yourself. Paste and post the images all over your world, including your bathroom mirror. Keep it in your face and top-of-mind.

Most people don't set long-term goals, let alone write them down. Some fear criticism if they are less than 100 percent successful. They believe that they have failed. Others don't know how to set goals. The vast majority do not appreciate the value of setting goals. I would like to repeat three words from the beginning of this section that summarize the benefits of written goals: **direction, momentum, and motivation.**

The Four Links of Effective Learning

You can significantly enrich your learning by incorporating the following building blocks.

1. Prepare & Organize

- Define your goal as outlined above. In Stephen Covey's book, *The 7 Habits of Highly Effective People*, his second habit is to *begin with the end in mind*.

- Identify your barriers and create a strategy to eliminate them. If you have a challenge finding barriers, review the *Be Aware of Obstructions to Your Learning* in the introduction to this book.

- Based on the goal that you set, declare your intention for each and every study or class session.

> *Wishing, hoping and goal setting*
> *cannot accomplish change without*
> *intention.*
>
> Author Dr. Wayne Dyer

- Generate some curiosity about the subject at hand. You can do this by brainstorming some wild and crazy questions – this primes the pump.

> *Curiosity is one of the permanent*
> *and certain characteristics of a*
> *vigorous mind.*
>
> Eighteenth century
> British essayist Samuel Johnson

- Examine the big picture. You can do this by creating a concept map of the lecture or chapter outline. *Mapping* is described in Chapter 1.

- Establish a positive study environment. Consider air, water, sound, light, privacy, and temperature. Finally, do a few *mind-body* exercises. (See Chapter 8.)

2. Attract the Information

- Write out what you already know.

- Even though class sessions don't afford you much control, if you are prepared with an outline concept map, you will be able to make, not just take, superior lecture notes. Remember, the brain is naturally associative, so it's always looking for links and connections. The concept map facilitates this.

- As suggested in the section on memory in the previous chapter, take frequent study breaks in order to maximize primacy and recency opportunities.

- In Chapter 10, you will find a technique called the "learning state." If you feel comfortable with that type of activity, embrace it.

3. *Practice, Elaborate, and Integrate*

- Repeated reviews entrench the information in your mind. Memory decay was discussed in the last chapter. One suggested review schedule is immediately as you return from a short break, then at one day, two days, one week, one month, and six months. These reviews are of just the key points and take a very short time to complete.

- Convene peer groups to challenge and thrash out, summarize and paraphrase, rehearse and present, simulate and role-play. The power here is that those with whom you collaborate most likely have learning styles, and therefore perceptions, differing from yours.

It is not because things are difficult
that we do not dare;
it is because we do not dare
that they are difficult.

Seneca the Elder

> *I dogmatise and I am contradicted, and in this conflict of opinions and sentiments I find delight.*
>
> Eighteenth century
> British essayist Samuel Johnson

- Explain your concept map to others.

- Play "What if?" Be creative by turning things upside-down and inside-out, play devil's advocate, or temporarily embrace a view opposite to your own.

- Produce a video or a song.

- Record yourself with a funny voice reading the lesson notes.

- Explain the subject to peers or younger siblings so that they can understand it.

- Convert your lesson to a "Jeopardy" game.

- Produce a flow chart and create flash cards.

- Create a mock test for a friend, and have a friend do the same for you.

4. Associate, Activate, and Archive

- As each lesson is completed, build a concept map of the complete course. You can work on this with your team of classmates.

- Your team can also discuss how the learning is relevant in the "real world".

- Debrief your efforts. What did you do well? What could you have done better?

Evaluating Training Effectiveness

In his 1994 book, *Evaluating Training Programs*, author Donald Kirkpatrick explained a four-level model to assess the efficacy of training, as follows. Although designed for the corporate world, academics may benefit from reading this.

1. Many of us have, at some point, attended a workshop where the trainer handed out a feedback sheet. This generally rates the reaction to the trainer, the venue, and the relevance to the participants. Positive feedback is usually insignificant. In contrast, negative feedback can influence how the material will be presented in the future. Information garnered at this level provides a foundation for designing the successive levels.

2. This level is intended to determine changes in skills, knowledge, or attitude. It may require pre- and post-tests. Results from this level provide information for the next level.

3.   This level seeks to determine if any changes have taken place in behavior. It is difficult, and sometimes impossible, to accurately gauge this outcome, since supervisor assessment and employee self-evaluations are subjective, each in their own way.

4.   This level seeks to detect changes in the company's bottom line. This is the most difficult to measure because of additional contributing factors. Has there been improved quality, increased production, increased sales, or decreased costs?

The purpose of this chapter was to bring to light some of the elements of accelerated learning, and give you a few tools to better equip you for your journey on this exciting path.

1.   **What is your greatest learning from this chapter?**

2.   **What is your greatest challenge with respect to setting and achieving goals?**

3.   **CALL TO ACTION:**
     Visit www.UnleashingBook.com to link to the CLI site. Choose the free self-coaching tool entitled "Goal Achiever." This tool will invite you to choose a specific goal, assist you in removing roadblocks to the achievement of that goal and provide you with solutions.

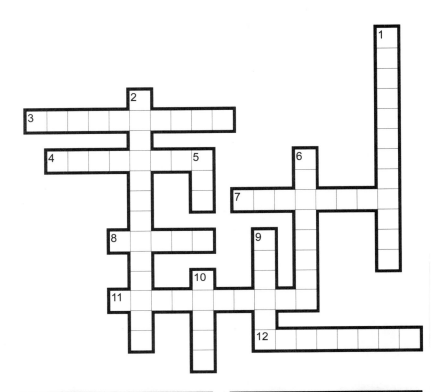

ACROSS

3. Last step in my goal–setting process
4. In goal–setting, assessment of your success must be _____
7. Newborns' brains are pre-programmed to perceive _____ and establish categories
8. They provide direction, momentum, and motivation
11. Traditional learning promotes standardization and strict _____
12. Goals without an action plan

DOWN

1. Conventional approaches to teaching are considered to be "brain _____"
2. This primes the pump
5. Begin with the _____ in mind
6. 4th Link: Associate, _____, and Archive
9. What you do after a short break, then at 1 day, 2 days, 1 week, one month, and six months
10. In learning, memory processes create _____ to associated information

BRILLIANT NOTES

YOUR MANY INTELLIGENCES

> *You have to find the place that you*
> *can shine, if you don't fit in with*
> *what everybody else is doing.*
>
> Cher

My first exposure to the concept of multiple intelligences was like a moment of revelation, a lights-flashing aha! moment with the last pieces of a difficult puzzle falling into place. Suddenly it was clear to me that effectively, each of us can learn using our own unique approach.

Consider intelligence as much more than a score on an IQ test. Understand that it determines and reflects how well we navigate through life's tasks and challenges.

Employees are frequently evaluated within the narrow scope of their job descriptions, without consideration of their potential in an enriched environment. Job enlargement and enrichment may offer opportunities for employees to exercise otherwise untapped resources. Both the employee and the company benefit.

Since students can learn and excel in many and various ways, teachers and schools would do well to go beyond long-held narrowly-focused practices of evaluating students mainly on their *verbal-linguistic* and *logical-mathematical* proficiencies. Students possessing these traits are rewarded with good grades from a school system based on century-old curricula that caters to the left-side of the brain. This narrow focus disenfranchises a large number of students, who must suffer at the hands of a structure wanting to fit square pegs into round holes. Perhaps relevant to this, and possibility in something of a plea for a broader perspective, Abraham Maslow once commented, "If the only tool you have is a hammer, every problem looks like a nail."

Although developed much earlier, the concept of multiple intelligences has been popularized by Professor Howard Gardner of Harvard University in his 1983 book, *Frames of Mind*, and by Tony Buzan in his book, *Head First*. This chapter will help prepare you to apply the accelerated learning techniques.

Apart from the verbal-linguistic and logical-mathematical types of intelligences mentioned above, other types, arguably just as important but often overlooked or downplayed, include *spatial, creative, bodily-kinesthetic, musical, social-interpersonal, spiritual-intrapersonal,* and *sensual-naturalistic*. Unfortunately, students who primarily express these traits have often been belittled or, at the very least, ignored.

Most types of intelligence are spread equally over both sexes; however, females tend to have a greater ability in linguistics, while males tend to dominate in the spatial and the logical-mathematical. Research at McMaster University has indicated that females have a greater density of neurons in that part of the brain associated with language, judgment, and planning future actions.[22] Research by Professor Jill M. Goldstein of Harvard Medical School, revealed that the parts of the brain involved in space perception are larger in men than in women.[23] This research may explain why men and women are drawn to different areas of endeavor; however, **you** have absolute control over **your** choices. If you have interest in a field that is not customary for your age, race, sex, height, shape, background, or education, just go for it. A robust enthusiasm, combined with action, will conquer seemingly insurmountable obstacles.

Most of us are a mixture of all the intelligences, usually displaying a particular aptitude for a few. Occasionally, there are cases where people develop a single strong intelligence without developing others, such as the character played by Dustin Hoffman in the role of the so-called idiot savant – in the movie *Rainman*, who displayed a pure logical-mathematical intelligence.

One of the ideals of education is the development of well-rounded individuals. In this direction, a traditional view of learners as being "empty vessels waiting to be filled with knowledge" is giving way to one that learners "continuously build understandings based on their prior experiences, external stimulation, and new information."

> *Education's purpose is to replace an empty mind with an open one.*
>
> Malcolm S. Forbes (1917 – 1990)
> Publisher – Forbes Magazine

A review of some of the intelligences, and strategies on how to develop them, follows here. As you read through each one, consider to what degree it applies to you. If you would like to delve more deeply into this subject, check Appendix 2 or our online links to recommended books.

*Remember always that you not only
have the right to be an individual,
you have an obligation to be one.*

Eleanor Roosevelt

Verbal-Linguistic Intelligence

The ability to speak well is valued in most societies. Skilled orators often rise to prominence in their professions. The written word has been with us for at least 6,000 years; oral communication has been part of humanity for almost 100,000 years. Complex oral tradition, passing on elaborate clan histories and myths, yarns, and fables, has been responsible for the perpetuation of culture through the generations.

True linguistic intelligence is more than just the ability to repeat questions on a standardized test. *Phonology* (sound), *syntax* (order), *semantics* (meaning), and *pragmatics* (context) are components of language use, and a highly linguistic person is able to employ them creatively, both in oral or written form. The capacity to use language to achieve practical goals and enhance lives is the most highly prized of the linguistic skills. People with superior linguistic skills typically include proofreaders, novelists, orators, political leaders, journalists, and speech writers, demonstrating talents with:

- *Phonology* – the clever use of puns, rhymes, tongue twisters, alliteration, and onomatopoeia.

- *Semantics* – deftly conveying nuance and shades of meaning.

- *Pragmatics* – to inspire, proselytize, entertain, instruct, and persuade.

Shoring Up Linguistic Abilities

Perhaps they might seem self-evident, or sometimes trivial, or perhaps for you, impracticable, but there are many steps you can take to build and hone your linguistic abilities. For example, you can read, journal, play word games such as Scrabble™ and crosswords, learn how to use a word processor, listen to recordings of orators, join Toastmasters or a similar group, volunteer to tutor someone in reading skills, attend a writer's seminar, and record and listen to your own voice.

All really great lovers are articulate, and verbal seduction is the surest road to actual seduction.

Writer & critic
Marya Mannes (1904 - 1990)

Logical-Mathematical Intelligence

Even though logical-mathematical intelligence is related to spatial, kinesthetic, linguistic, and musical elements, it has unique properties that act as core components.

Early-childhood logical brain programming deals with concrete objects through sensory contact, cause and effect, and numbers. As a person reaches adolescence, thoughts become more deductive and hypothetical. Systematic operational reasoning, though not employed by the majority of adults, is a skill that may be acquired. A collection of problem-solving strategies is known as the field of *heuristics*, which includes such techniques as finding analogies, exploring problems parallel to what's being worked on, dissecting a problem, proposing a possible solution and working backward, generalization, specialization, and assuming the opposing view. Sharpening these skills will make us not only better problem solvers, but also better communicators.

It is important at this juncture to clarify that this intelligence does not include the manipulation of numbers through memorized algorithms and formulas without an understanding of the logic behind them. These rote mathematical proficiencies are achieved through mental calculations and are due to a highly developed linguistic capacity. To be truly *numerate* (literate with numbers) in the real world, is to be competent in problem solving, probability, estimation, and statistics.

Studies show that a person's income in the first decade of work correlates positively to the number of math courses taken in school. Those with a poor number sense are subject to the evils of misleading advertising, and may have unrealistic expectations in all areas of life, from home budgeting to lotteries. At a macro level, an innumerate society operates with the disadvantage of inadequately understanding economic, political, and social issues.

Another aspect of this intelligence is scientific literacy. The wonderment of science that children possess is often dampened by curricula requiring memorization of laws and formulas. Granted, memorization provides valuable exercise for the brain, resulting in neural growth, but often at the expense of a passion for science. One informal survey of Harvard graduates showed that only two of the twenty-three interviewees were able to satisfactorily explain why it is hotter in the summer than in the winter. A survey conducted at Northern Illinois University indicated that over 93 percent of adults lacked a fundamental knowledge of scientific vocabulary and methodology, and demonstrated a poor understanding of the impact of science on the world. Scientific illiteracy may diminish people's ability to intelligently evaluate government and corporate initiatives.

People with good logical-mathematical skills typically include scientists, researchers, detectives, lawyers, and accountants.

Developing Logical-Mathematical Intelligence

Here are some ideas for developing your logical-mathematical intelligence. Play with brain teasers and puzzles, take a science or math course, read about math and science discoveries, learn a computer programming language, watch the science-discovery channel, visit a museum, aquarium or observatory, and teach math or science concepts to someone with less knowledge.

Spatial Intelligence

For processing information, 15 percent of the general population is highly visual; another 15 percent does not regularly use visual images; the remaining 70 percent falls somewhere in between.

Some people accept their first impression of what they perceive. They depend mainly on their linguistic or logical-mathematical intelligence to operate in their personal and business environments. This approach, which depends on symbol systems, limits the potential richness of their world by restricting their observation to superficial evidence.

Every child is an artist.
The problem is how to remain an
artist once one grows up.

Pablo Picasso

Those who are able to reframe, reinterpret, re-evaluate, and consider alternative levels of significance are considered spatially intelligent. They have a keen eye for relationships of line, direction, shape, volume, space, balance, shadow, harmony, pattern, and color. Among those who express spatial intelligence are artists, navigators, chess players, battlefield strategists, architects, mechanics, engineers, land surveyors, aboriginal trackers, airline pilots, and even the Sherpas of Nepal.

Enhancing Spatial Intelligence

There is a whole host of ways for enhancing spatial intelligence. Learn how to build a house of cards, draw, study still-photo and movie composition, experience orienteering, learn an ideographic language such as Chinese, and learn how to interpret or create flowcharts and concept maps (See Chapter 1). Incorporate graphics in reports, study optical illusions, and interview mechanical engineers or artists.

Musical Intelligence

For millennia, societies have passed down their genealogical history, navigational data, anthologies, and culture to the succeeding generations through folklore, much of which was transmitted via song and music. During the middle ages, monasteries used music to facilitate the memorization of scriptures by the monks. In aid of memorizing the alphabet, schoolchildren sing their ABC's, and chant the times-tables to burn them into their brain. Advertisers have long appreciated the value of jingles, and national anthems are tools designed to emotionally inspire loyalty.

Children have an ability to hear musical tones in their heads. Unless they grow up to be musicians, composers, or recording technicians, they lose much of this auditory eidetic imaging aptitude through lack of rehearsal. Adults who are prepared to practice can recapture that ability.

Several research studies have shown that background music will boost creativity through brain-wave activation. Whether one is stressed or simply experiencing a mental block, music can release the impasse. Music counter-balances all the left-brain activities experienced in the modern world. The power of music has long been recognized by so-called primitive cultures. In order to generate trance states for cultural and religious ceremonies, they have harnessed the power of ritual drumming, chanting, rocking, singing, and dancing. Some religions still use these techniques to this day.

Music can stimulate motor skills, language, and vocabulary. In classrooms and corporate training rooms alike, it can improve discipline, rapport, and attention spans. It can foster more focused groups and aid in soothing hyperactivity. Studies show that inserting music into the learning situation brings distinct improvement in mathematics, science, and reading. Playing or listening to music creates new neural pathways that actually train the brain for higher forms of thinking. One example is spatial-temporal reasoning, which is creating mental images and thinking ahead in space and time; this shows up in chess, music, and math.

A 1998 study investigated the psychological impact of four types of music: *grunge rock, classical, new age,* and *designer.*

The analysis of their "before and after" psychological profiles showed mixed results for new age and classical music. Subjects exposed to grunge rock exhibited signs of increased hostility, sadness, tension, fatigue, and reduced caring, relaxation, mental clarity, and vigor. For those subjects exposed to music designed to have specific effects on the listener (i.e. designer music), significant increases were measured in mental clarity, caring, relaxation, and vigor. At the same time, negative feelings such as hostility, fatigue, sadness, and tension decreased.[24]

Dr. Paul MacLean of the National Institute of Mental Health said, "The emotional or limbic system of the brain is so powerful that it can either facilitate or inhibit learning and higher order thinking skills. Listening to music appears to involve the brain at almost every level, even evoking emotional feelings. Using both the cortex and limbic systems can enhance long-term learning."[25]

> *Music is a mortal law.*
> *It gives soul to the universe,*
> *wings to the mind, flight to the*
> *imagination, and charm and gaiety*
> *to life and to everything.*
>
> Plato

Examples of people who have excellent musical intelligence are composers, recording engineers, piano-tuners, music instrument makers, singers, and performers.

Psychologist Georgi Lozanov developed methods of learning languages through the use of Baroque music in a specific formula. (See *Suggestopedia* in Chapter 12.)

Cultivating One's Musical Intelligence

Join a choir or recreational sing-along group, take formal music or singing lessons, play musical games, sing in the shower, take a music appreciation course, play background music, attend lectures by experts such as Wayne Perry or Dick Sutphen, listen carefully to rhythms of life, such as traffic, birds, and machinery, rediscover the songs of childhood, listen to a heartbeat, experience the excitement of aboriginal drumming, and read biographies of famous singers and composers.

Bodily-Kinesthetic Intelligence

During the first two years of life, virtually all thinking takes place through the body. Swiss child researcher Jean Piaget calls this the *sensory-motor* stage of cognitive development. Infants construct their image of the world by grasping, crawling, and tasting. The physical actions gradually become internalized as the children grow and gain control over their body. This internalized circuitry provides the key to building many levels of abstraction for future creative thinking.

The ancient Greeks valued gymnastics for cultivating the powers of the mind. Over the succeeding centuries, however many cultures created and perpetuated a rift between body and mind, by emphasizing logical-mathematical and linguistic skills. In the West, the intelligentsia relegated physical pursuits to crafts, manual labor, sports, and sex. The Judeo-Christian tradition has promoted a separation of mind and body. On the other hand, the eastern philosophies have always pursued the development of the mind-body through tai chi, aikido, and yoga. In the West, only within the past few decades has the mind been considered a factor in sports excellence.

Thinking, learning, and memory are distributed throughout the body. Much of the learning, thinking, and decision-making take place on the cellular and molecular level.[26] The body and mind come together as a completely integrated bio-electro-chemical system.

People who express great bodily-kinesthetic intelligence include dancers, race car drivers, jockeys, mime artists, surgeons, actors, athletes, some inventors, and outdoor workers.

The Bane of Kinesthetic Learners

Conventional teaching methods confine learners to chairs, thereby depriving them of numerous opportunities to stimulate the brain. There is a growing belief that many children are misdiagnosed as ADHD (Attention Deficit Hyperactivity Disorder) and prescribed Ritalin or some other amphetamines.

> *The way children are treated in schools is sheer madness. Those who can't sit still are stuck with the hyperactive label and treated as anomalies and frequently drugged.*
>
> Author Edward T. Hall:
> *Beyond Culture* (1976)

It is becoming widely accepted in the counseling field that some children are being cavalierly misdiagnosed as ADD and ADHD. Alternative factors accounting for the symptoms being exhibited may be PTSD due to family upheaval, seizures, medications (prescription or otherwise), thyroid disorders, writing difficulties, hearing and vision problems, gifted children who might be bored in school, autism, mental retardation, simple peer or teacher personality conflicts, lead poisoning and anemia, learning disabilities, depression, allergies, and sleep disturbances.

The Benefits of Being Kinesthetic Learners

The part of the brain responsible for fine movements throughout the body is next to the part dealing with decision-making and thinking. Many youngsters are kinesthetic learners, and involving tactile, hands-on guidance, known as *somatic learning*, can supercharge their education. (See Chapter 12 about Total Physical Response.) Kinesthetic intelligence includes artistic endeavors, skilled trades, and specialized physical activities, which are not necessarily linked to logical-mathematical and linguistic output. They are unique intelligences in their own right.

The term *haptic personality* describes people who receive information primarily from kinesthetic sources. The term's originator, art educator Viktor Lowenfeld, explained that the haptic types use muscular sensations, kinesthetic experiences, touch impressions, and all the experiences of self to establish their relationship to the outside world.

Twenty-five percent of people possess a keen ability to accurately have a "gut" feeling about situations, places, and people.

Dr. Tad James of Advanced Neuro Dynamics teaches a simple technique that allows a person to tap into previously-learned information that is seemingly inaccessible to the conscious mind. When something is studied, it resides in the subconscious mind. The technique is called "sticky." It involves rubbing the index finger against a plastic surface, or the adjoining thumb. The difference in friction when thinking *yes* or *no* may then be used to determine answers in true/false and multiple choice questions.

Effects of Activity and Good Posture

Eastern cultures have long understood the psychophysical value of specific postures, such as in yoga. Educators increasingly appreciate the importance of posture in its effect on academic performance, as it relates to the flow of oxygen-rich blood to the brain. Dramatic improvements in cognitive functioning have been seen during research in the British school system. Anecdotal evidence has indicated that physical movement, such as walking or running, can boost cognitive ability. Formal research by scientists in the Veterans Administration Medical Center in Salt Lake City and the Oregon Health Sciences Center has demonstrated that exercise enhances memory, improves reaction times, and aids in the generation of unique and spontaneous ideas.

Methods To Develop Bodily-Kinesthetic Intelligence

Join a sports group, learn a craft such as woodworking or sculpting, take lessons in yoga, exercise regularly, be led around blindfolded, create a collection of textures, play charades, receive a deep tissue massage, develop eye-hand coordination through sports, take a mime class, and learn how to conduct a Japanese tea ceremony. (See Chapter 10 on NLP about *Kinesthetic Learners* and Chapter 8 on *Mind-body* exercises.)

Social-Interpersonal Intelligence

Social cognition is the ability to make fine distinctions in the intentions, motivations, moods, feelings, and thoughts of others. As a child becomes an adult, social interactions carve out cognitive maps containing stereotypes, beliefs, fixed responses, attitudes, and behavioral patterns. While some of these traits, expectations, and schemata are valid and serve us well, others are discriminatory and counterproductive.

Talking about oneself can also be a means to conceal oneself.

Friedrich Wilheim Nietzsche

According to the results of research by behavioral scientists, the most decisive factor influencing career advancement for executives is their ability or inability to comprehend other people's perspectives. Unlike most of the world's societies, which are naturally collaborative in social and business transactions, the western cultures have tended to be competitive. Slowly but surely, western business and academia are beginning to experiment with teamwork and collaborative projects;

for instance, the adoption of Japanese *quality circles* in the North American car-manufacturing industry, where workers periodically meet to discuss problems and offer suggestions. On the social plane, research has shown that the richer the social network a person has, the greater that person's longevity.

> *A lack of social relationships constitutes a major risk for mortality.*
>
> James S. House,
> Chair, Sociology Department
> University of Michigan

Nonverbal communication has been estimated to account for anywhere from 60 percent to 90 percent of information transmitted between people. Humans are hard-wired to gesture while speaking; children, blind since birth, instinctively gesture when they speak, even while speaking to another blind person. Experts estimate that there are five thousand distinct hand gestures, a thousand different postures, and a quarter-million facial expressions. There also exists an abundant array of patterns for factors like distances between people, touching, and eye contact. Research has revealed that one person intentionally making an emotive expression can yield the equivalent emotion in another. As mentioned in Chapter 2, emotional body language is universal; a number of other signals, on the other hand, are non-emotional (culturally-based) and subject to gross misinterpretation, (for instance, it is highly rude to expose the bottom of one's foot in Arab countries). Reading body language begins in infancy. Before they are even two years old, babies will know every mood and gesture of their caretakers. They learn very early what buttons to push and when. They know when to demand, when to back off, and when to act submissively.

Interpersonal skills fall into four skill areas: *listening, assertiveness* (see below), *conflict-resolution,* and *collaboration.* They are not necessarily innate; they can be learned. Stephen Covey's fifth habit, "Seek first to understand; then to be understood," supports all four of these skills.[27] Without criticism, genuine openness to the other's view breaks down barriers and opens the lines of communication. Interactive techniques such as an encouraging posture, appropriate eye contact and gestures, legitimate and constructive questioning, authentic paraphrasing, and supporting the other's ego are vital for consensus and resolution.

Listen...
or your tongue will keep you deaf.

A Native American saying

In her book, *Body-Centered Coaching*, Marlena Field said:

> Empowered listening is a way of being, a way of being fully present – body, mind and spirit. Empowered listening is being curious and paying attention to our clients without anything else interfering in the process. With empowered listening we will hear the essence of what is being said and find ourselves whole-heartedly open to our intuition and creativity. We will be more present and receptive and be more natural, appropriate and creative with our responses. It is empowering for both people.

> *O, it is excellent to have a giant's strength, but it is tyrannous to use it like a giant.*
>
> William Shakespeare

My experience is that many people confuse assertiveness with aggression. *Aggressive* behavior is when people protect their own rights, **without** taking into account the rights of others. *Assertiveness* is defending one's own rights, while concurrently **considering** the rights of others. *Non-assertive* people **do not defend** their own rights and, as a result, allow others to take advantage of them. What about the person who steps out of an elevator and just stands there, oblivious to those behind who want to get out. That's the *Passive-Aggressive*.

Those who should typically show fine interpersonal intelligence include politicians, managers, sales people, counselors, religious leaders, bartenders, waiters/waitresses, teachers, front desk staff, and publicists.

Generating Greater "People Smarts":

Proactively expand your social network, volunteer, practice active listening, join an internet chat room, perform random acts of kindness to total strangers, observe body language in social interactions, join a hiking club, and take a course in communication skills.

Spiritual-Intrapersonal Intelligence

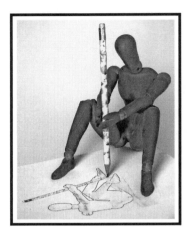

A sense of *self* has always puzzled and intrigued humans. As far back as 500 BC, Buddhist philosophers regarded the self as a concept that was non-tangible in nature. Their concept of self included thoughts, feelings, sensations, and ideas. Cognitive psychologists have now relabeled this description as a very complex mental map that facilitates our understanding of the world around us. It is the nucleus of our creativity, vitality, spontaneity, and emotions.

Each of us has within us a source of understanding and wisdom that knows who we are, where we have been, and where we are going. It is in tune with our unfolding purpose, and senses clearly the next steps to be taken to fulfill this purpose.

The Psychosynthesis & Education Trust

Those who have solid intrapersonal intelligence generally include counselors, novelists, wise elders, philosophers, researchers, and mystics.

Many categories of *self* have common characteristics, and there is value in exploring them. By understanding their distinctiveness, we may gain a clearer picture of how we fit into the world. Knowing and understanding ourselves gives us a better understanding of our learning style.

Self-Esteem

Also known as *self-worth,* a person's self-esteem is forged during the first seven or eight years of life. By then the mind has created the *critical faculty* (also known as the critical factor) to filter incoming messages, thus protecting the impressionable and immature subconscious. Until that is in place, absolutely everything a child hears, sees, and experiences will fashion a core belief that could be a lifetime guide.

If, during this critical period, a child consistently hears, "You are so disorganized, you'll never amount to anything," or similar judgmental put-downs, there is a strong possibility that the person will experience self-sabotage in later life. In *transactional analysis*, the core belief is known as the *parent* and it relentlessly directs behavior. Low self-esteem is created in an atmosphere of conditional love and subsequently reinforced through negative self-talk. Unfortunately, contrary evidence is usually disregarded.

Some people endeavor to bolster their self-esteem through external elements, like marriage, alliance with others, and even the accumulation of money, titles, and degrees. While surrounding oneself with positive people has its benefits, it is problematic to define the self through external trappings.

Although it is a good thing to be proud of accomplishments, it is essential for people to make a clear distinction between their identities and their accomplishments.

All other "selves" emanate from self-esteem, that is, they take cues from the quality of the self-esteem. A fragile self-esteem will spawn weakness. A sound self-esteem, built in an environment of unconditional love, will sponsor resilient self-identities.

> *Don't let your ego get too close*
> *to your position, so that if your*
> *position gets shot down,*
> *your ego doesn't go with it.*
>
> Colin Powell
> Former U.S. Secretary of State

> *Trust yourself.*
> *You know more than you think.*
>
> Dr. Benjamin Spock

Self-Awareness

Self-awareness is the ability to reflect on our thought processes. We can become aware of many signals received from our bodies. We are not our feelings, thoughts, behaviors, and moods. These are simply processes that we experience and are not a "part" of our essence. We are able to objectively scrutinize the way we see ourselves. This social mirror of our place within humankind allows us to evaluate the roles of nature and nurture in our own attitudes and behaviors.

Self-Acceptance

Self-acceptance is the coming to terms with who we are right now, just as we are – with all our faults, weaknesses, and errors, as well as our assets and strengths. It is important to appreciate that the negatives **belong to us** – they are **not us**. Recognition of shortcomings is a healthy first step in personal growth. The actual self is necessarily imperfect and dynamically striving for improvement. It is always a work-in-progress. Blatantly professing to be perfect produces great mental strain.

Self-Honesty

Self-honesty is being in touch with one's own basic human instincts for justice and fairness for self and others. It means being aware of rationalizations used to counter our conscience and other internal signals. It means ridding oneself of the need to appraise self-worth in external terms. It also means assessing one's strengths and weaknesses realistically.

Self-Image

Self-image is a custom-built collage fabricated from how we think others see us. We tend to draw conclusions about ourselves based on how we are treated. Psychologists generally agree that people underrate themselves. An inner sense of mastery and competence is developed only when we focus on our inner core of personal vitality and creativity rather than on seemingly negative evidence.

Negative feedback can be constructive in helping us get back on course; however, when we obsess about what others think, we relentlessly and consciously monitor every act, word, and manner. This creates inhibited, self-conscious perfectionists.

Historically, when employees demonstrated loyalty and hard work, they had an expectation of job security, regular pay increases, and promotions. Now, in many work locations, uncertainty and stress prevail. Habitual feelings of injustice lead to the victim mode of resentment and self-pity, thus lowering self-image and self-esteem.

Self-Mastery

Self-mastery is the knowledge about how to manage oneself on a daily basis so as to maximize accomplishment. Remember the old saying, "By failing to plan, people plan to fail." Setting goals that are specific, timely, achievable, measurable, accountable, and realistic, and which demand just a slight stretch, have the likelihood of being reached, if combined with passion and action.

One constant in life is change. How we manage change depends on our experience and mind-set. An unpleasant encounter may subconsciously program us to either shy away from, or preferably, relish a new challenge. It all depends on how we perceive the original event. Some of my clients are "stuck" in their jobs, their relationships, or their lives in general. By remaining in their comfort zone, they are denying themselves opportunities to live at their full capacity. Self-mastery is knowing when to learn new skills or take on new responsibilities, when to hold on to beliefs that serve you, and when to let go of beliefs that do not serve you. (See Chapter 3 on Goal-setting.)

When I was a sales representative, I used to look forward to calling on this one particular company because the visit never failed to raise my spirits. One of their top managers always displayed an upbeat attitude that obviously permeated the organization. I would say, "Hi John... how's it going?" and no matter how the day seemed to be going, his answer would always be an enthusiastic, "TERR-RRIF-IC!" These monthly encounters have had a positive and lasting effect on me. Thank you John Henry.

From that point on, when the "rainy days and Mondays always get me down" people were around me, I poured on the good cheer. Think about it. If you maintain a consistently happy disposition, you will stick out from the crowd – in a good way.

Self-Efficacy

Self-efficacy is the context-specific assessment of belief in our personal capabilities to organize and execute what is required so as to achieve the intended goal. It is concerned not with the skills we have, but rather with our control over our own level of functioning. People with high self-efficacy choose more demanding tasks. They set higher goals, put in more effort, and persist longer than those who are low in self-efficacy.

Dr. Albert Bandura of Stanford University said, "People's **beliefs** about their abilities have a profound effect on those abilities. Ability is not a fixed property; there is a huge variability in how you perform. People who have a sense of self-efficacy bounce back from failures; they approach things in terms of how to handle them rather than worrying about what can go wrong." (The emphasis is mine.)

Self-efficacy grows through personal and vicarious experience, discipline, and valid feedback. Although usually considered in a single context, there may also be a generalized effect reflecting a person's abilities across a broad array of difficult or novel situations. For instance, if someone is loved by a supportive family on the home front, then that person will display a greater confidence on the job. This will be reflected by peer and management feedback, which will, in turn, show up on the home front, perpetuating the cycle.

Success is the ability to go from one failure to another with no loss of enthusiasm.

Winston Churchill

Self-Confidence

Self-confidence is an external manifestation of the health of self-esteem, self-efficacy, and self-mastery. Although it reflects the strength of these selves, it can be purposefully overridden to become a façade that we deliberately create for external scrutiny. I had a client who was a television actor. He once told me that actors often don't know where their next job is coming from. They may seem to possess a great deal of self-confidence, but often it hides a shaky self-esteem.

If the façade is merely bravado, it is shallow. The technique of "act-as-if" can have a positive effect on the subconscious, since it cannot differentiate between something real and something vividly imagined.

Self-Love

Self-love is the regard you have for your own happiness. It parallels unconditional love inasmuch as, no matter what you do, you nurture yourself by giving yourself permission to take pleasure in whatever life has to offer. In the therapy of Emotional Freedom Technique (EFT – as discussed in Chapter 5), we use the phrase, "I deeply and completely love and accept myself."

Self-Actualization

Self-actualization is the realization of one's full potential through creativity, independence, spontaneity, and a grasp and appreciation of this world.

There were three brick-layers at work.

Each of them was asked in turn – "What are you doing?"

The first brick-layer answered, "I'm laying bricks."

The second answered, "My job... to support my family."

And the third bricklayer smiled and said, "Me? Why, I'm building the world's most magnificent cathedral."

Developing Intrapersonal Intelligence

Learn and then practice meditation, listen to motivational or inspirational tapes and CDs, regularly record and self-analyze dreams, take a self-hypnosis class, write a journal and/or autobiography, start a new business, take an aptitude test, set short-term and long-term goals and work on them, learn about transactional analysis, enhance self-esteem through positive self-talk and affirming successes, learn more about the self through being familiar with various schools of psychology, pray, keep a mirror handy to study self while in different moods, and do your best to associate only with positive people.

Naturalistic Intelligence

This intelligence facility goes beyond technical knowledge of flora and fauna. It indicates an inherent compassion and consciousness for all living things. Examples of people who have exhibited this trait are Jane Goodall, Charles Darwin, and Pulitzer Prize winner and naturalist, E. O. Wilson. It is intriguing to note that city-bound children may transfer their naturalist tendencies to discriminate and appreciate different types of cars, buildings, or clothing. This intelligence can be enhanced through political or social activity for preservation of nature, hiking in the wilderness, exploring a backyard or parkland, researching online or in an encyclopedia, growing a garden, and reading biographies of naturalists.

The whole purpose of education is to turn mirrors into windows.

Author Sydney J. Harris

How Intelligence
Relates to Accelerated Learning

It is essential to keep in mind that each of us is a unique mix of intelligences. Some intelligences are stronger and so have greater profiles than others. Apart from simply being aware of which intelligences are stronger, learners, both corporate and academic, can boost their effectiveness by applying the wealth of tools that each intelligence supplies. These will principally come into focus in the *Practice, Elaborate, and Integrate* period of learning discussed earlier. Go back now to the Four Links of Effective Learning in Chapter 3 and identify which intelligences are being employed in each of the strategies.

One final intelligence, which is not ordinarily included in this concept, is Emotional Intelligence. I've included it in the next chapter on Emotions.

1. **What is your greatest learning from this chapter?**

2. **What personal successes could you celebrate at this very moment in your life?**

3. **CALL TO ACTION:**
   Visit www.UnleashingBook.com to link to the CLI site. Choose the free self-coaching tool entitled "The Brain Walk® – Value Amplification." This tool will invite you to select a value in which you are already strong i.e. giving respect, honesty. Next, the tool will assist you in amplifying that value, giving you the ability to become even stronger in it.

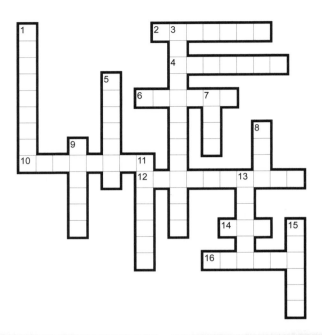

A C R O S S

2. Developer of Multiple Intelligence Theory
4. Learning by doing (tactile, hands-on)
6. 60-90% of information transmitted between people is non-_____
10. Being competent in problem-solving, probability, estimation, and statistics
12. Clever use of puns, rhymes, tongue twisters is _____ intelligence
14. Dustin Hoffman character in Rainman
16. Intelligence is not an _____ score

D O W N

1. Social _____: Ability to make fine distinctions in the intentions of others
3. Sticking up for yourself & considering rights of others
5. Ability to reframe and re-evaluate is _____ intelligence
7. Kinesthetic learners are misdiagnosed as this
8. Music is the counter-balance to _____ brain activities.
9. Exercise enhances _____ & improves reaction times
11. The body and mind are a completely integrated bio-_____-chemical system
13. Only one strong intelligence is idiot _____
15. Self-worth = self-_____

BRILLIANT NOTES

EMOTIONS, FEELINGS, AND LEARNING

> *Better keep yourself clean and bright; you are the window through which you must see the world*
>
> George Bernard Shaw

Body, thought, and emotion are intimately blended through complex nerve networks, and function in concert to shape our awareness. Emotions interpret, arrange, direct, and summarize information received through the five senses. They color our perception of the world and we often unconsciously react to them. They are primary and universal survival tools that permit us to experience joy, surprise, sadness, fear, disgust, or threat. Since emotions are linked to survival, they receive neurological message priority. This chapter will provide insight into just how our feelings and emotions impact the quality of our learning.

Are emotions and feelings the same thing? The difference is that feelings are not linked to survival. Furthermore, they are context-specific responses shaped by the environment, culture, and society. Emotions can be measured through variations in blood pressure, heart rate variability, brain-imaging techniques, and electro-dermal response. Feelings are difficult to measure. Some examples of feelings are frustration, anticipation, jealousy, cynicism, worry, and optimism. In the present context, I have reason for being particular about this distinction, though most people lump these together for convenience.

Emotions are...the function where mind and body most closely and mysteriously interact.

Ronald de Sousa, Author
The Rationality of Emotion

Decoding the Stress Factor

Traumatic events and enduring stress can take a toll on a person's physical and psychological health. The memory and accompanying negative emotions of a stressful incident or condition, at any point in life, can lay dormant for years. When triggered by some later stressful event, they can evoke negative beliefs, desires, fantasies, compulsions, obsessions, addictions, or dissociation. This toxic brew can inhibit learning and memory, and generally fracture human wholeness. Unless the person feels emotionally secure, it is almost impossible for the "thinking" parts of the brain (neo-cortex and frontal lobes) to function effectively.

All living things are created with built-in defense mechanisms. The human version is a fight-or-flight reaction to perceived threats. Stressors, whether sudden and unexpected or consistent and ongoing, trigger this natural effect. Most people are unaware of the common causes and the long-term effects of stress.

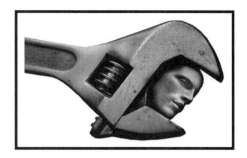

Stress is cumulative, and the effects of substantial stress are dissipated only after a period of twelve to eighteen months. Low-level consistent stress keeps the body in a constant fight-or-flight stance. This means that the *mind-body* is not able to operate at maximum performance. In order to maintain this steady defense mode, energy is diverted away from both the immune system and the brain. Stress and constant fear, at any age, create a chemical imbalance, which can confuse the brain's normal circuits.

> *The time to relax is*
> *when you don't have time for it.*
> Author Sydney J. Harris

Chronic Conditions

A person's physical and emotional well-being is closely linked to the ability to effectively act, think, and learn. Long-term exposure to threat, conflict, or humiliation will damage self-esteem and may result in a condition known as *learned helplessness*. This chronic defensive posture is characterized by a vortex of negative emotions, self-limiting beliefs, apathy, anxiety, fear, mistrust, immature coping behaviors, and a diminished interest

and ability to process information. This state is context-specific
and can be triggered over and over by contact with a certain
teacher, peer, subject, building, or memory.

An unusual physiological effect occurs during emotionally-
stressful conditions. As a reflex response to a threat, the eyes
move peripherally so that they can monitor a greater field of
vision. This makes it virtually impossible for the eyes to track
across a page of writing. Enduring stress will strengthen the
muscles of the outer eye, making central focus and tracking
a permanent problem. A condition of traumatized children is
called "wall-eye" where both eyes are locked in a sustained
distrustful peripheral focus. This condition can be overcome
through whole-brain integration exercises. (See Chapter 8; also
the *learning state* in *PhotoReading*™, Chapter 11.)

Emotional Manifestations

There are many theories on emotions. According to Leslie
Cameron-Bandler, author of *Emotional Hostage: Rescuing Your
Emotional Life*, it is possible to experience 421 emotions, from
rage to peace of mind. Emotion is literally energy in motion. As
mentioned in the earlier section on the limbic system, emotions
and external behavior influence one another. Behavior, whether
desirable or not, is often a manifestation of our emotions. And
since the mind-body is one system, the reverse is true; emotion
affects physiology.

Emotions influence perception and learning. In her book, *Molecules of Emotions*, Dr. Candace Pert wrote: "The brain filters our perceptions to create our 'reality'. The decisions about what we perceive, remember, and learn are regulated by emotion — the interaction of peptides and receptors in the brain. At the same time, emotions are a response to this filtered reality, memories, and learning." Certain positive emotions and feelings act as catalysts to learning. Curiosity, appreciation, and calmness enable receptivity and inhibit resistance. High self-esteem and self-confidence boost the learning process. Our innate personality types can indicate how we are apt to deal with the range of situations that life offers, and in which environments we are most comfortable. (See section on *Styles and Learning Strategies* in Chapter 7.)

Emotional Intelligence

Psychologist and author Daniel Goleman PhD studied the influence of emotions in people's lives. His theory, *Emotional Intelligence* (EI), maintains that the key to success at school, at work, or in the family is **emotion** and that the traditional IQ (Intelligence Quotient) is too narrow in focus since it measures only left-brain intelligence and is highly biased in favor of the Western World in design. (See Chapter 4 on *Intelligences*). Dr. Goleman suggests that the IQ be replaced by EQ (Emotional Quotient) or EIQ (Emotional Intelligence Quotient). Not to be confused with the variety of intelligences covered in chapter 4, Dr. Goleman asserts, "Emotional Intelligence is a master aptitude, a capacity that profoundly affects all other abilities, either facilitating or interfering with them."

According to Dr. Goleman, rather than being an inherited trait, EI is a completely learned phenomenon. That is nurtured through upbringing, and exposure to people and situations. Emotionally intelligent people excel in life, and have flourishing relationships and careers. They have an excellent ability to marshal their emotional impulses and learn to delay gratification. They have the self-awareness to know what they are feeling, and are able to think about and express these emotions. They have empathy for the feelings of others and insight into how others think. They are optimistic and generally positive. They understand easily the dynamics of a given group and, more importantly, where they fit inside that group.

Low EI can sabotage the intellect and ruin educational endeavors, relationships, and careers. The greatest impact may be on the children of people with low EI who fall prey to depression, eating disorders, aggressiveness, and even crime. Emotional Intelligence can be nurtured and strengthened through training and/or therapy. A number of innovative techniques exist to transform negative emotions into positive ones. See this book's web site for a link to this resource.

Tools to Positively Affect Emotions

Natural Light

Research has demonstrated that exposure to natural light has a positive effect on human health, emotional well-being, and therefore learning. Some of the common symptoms of lack of natural light are fatigue, disturbed sleep patterns, appetite and weight disorders, depression, skin damage, and suppressed immune functions. During the short days of winter, a common problem is *Seasonal Affective Disorder* (SAD). The symptoms can be easily remedied through daily exposure to sunlight. Alternatively, *Bright Light Therapy* (phototherapy), using a minimum of ten thousand lux units for thirty minutes in the early morning, will often cure SAD. Just to put this into perspective, even the cloudiest day is rarely below ten thousand lux, and a sunny afternoon could be as much as one-hundred thousand lux. Do your own research to understand the current technology for Bright Light Therapy devices.

The commonly-used fluorescent tubes, found in many offices and training facilities, have only narrow spectrum light, and they also emit a constant pulsing that can create stress and fatigue. A study of 750 classrooms (21,000 students) in California, Washington, and Colorado found that students in classrooms with windows and skylights learned 20 to 26 percent faster than students in classrooms with the least natural light exposure. A Florida study of two first grade classrooms found that full-spectrum lighting reduced nervousness and hyperactivity. The students also improved their overall classroom performance.[28]

The Law Of Emotion

A person can only have one set of emotions and feelings at a time. Stronger emotions and feelings replace weaker ones. Indifference or boredom can be substituted with appreciation or curiosity. Curiosity can then be replaced with excitement, which in turn can enable a high-energy learning state. Self-criticism can be substituted with a strong self-esteem. *Neurolinguistic Programming* (NLP) is a way of modeling how successful people achieve their results. It gives us a wonderful set of tools and principles for enhancing the components of *emotional intelligence*: self-awareness, self-control, motivation, empathy, and social skills. (See *NLP* in Chapter 10.)

The Love Factor

Two parallel studies were conducted on young newborn rats sourced from the same supplier. All aspects of the experiments were identical, including their food. In one of the locations, Cambridge University in England, the rats were gaining weight and thriving. In the other location, Harvard University in the USA, the rats were experiencing less measurable growth.

The researchers were unable to rationalize the difference until they later discovered the one factor that made the difference.

In order to clean the cages at Harvard, the maintenance staff moved the rats into other cages. At Cambridge, while some maintenance workers cleaned the cages, other workers held and stroked the rats. If TLC (tender loving care) can have that kind of effect on the physiology of rats, think what it can do for a human mind.

HeartMath®

When our body and mind are in balance, our inner systems function with a higher degree of synchronization, efficiency and harmony. This state correlates with improved emotional stability, quality of emotional experience, health, and cognitive performance.

Perceptions underlie how we think and feel about the matters with which we are dealing. Our thoughts, and especially the emotions related to what we perceive, cause numerous physiological changes in our bodies. These variations can be observed in the nervous system, the hormonal system, and the cardio-vascular system. They then feed back and affect the brain's neural circuitry, and this looping continues unless redirected through intervention.

Neural pathways in the brain and body are developed and reinforced by the degree to which they are exercised. Reinforcing either a healthy response or a stressful reaction is, in actuality, "hard-wiring" the relevant pattern into the nervous system. The heart has a complex nervous system that has been described as being its own "brain" with an intricate circuitry that enables it to act independently, learn, and remember. The information sent from the heart to the brain can have profound effects on the higher brain centers by influencing perception, emotion, and learning. Through the use of heart rhythm analysis, researchers have been able to observe the effects of even more subtle emotions and feelings, such as frustration, worry and anxiety, love, care, compassion and appreciation.

Institute of HeartMath®

Research by the Institute of HeartMath has revealed that emotions and feelings are reflected in unique heart rhythm patterns. The measure of these beat-to-beat changes in heart rate is known as *heart rate variability* (HRV). When these patterns are shared with the higher brain centers, they hugely affect the way the brain processes information. Feelings of frustration and anxiety cause the heart rhythms to become more disordered and irregular, causing energy drains, insecurities, and ambiguity in decision-making. Feelings of love and appreciation increase clear and effective thinking, problem solving, discernment, and memory recall. This is because high quality emotions generate more ordered and coherent heart rhythms, which in turn, reduce nervous system chaos and facilitate cortical function.

The Institute of HeartMath has developed a biofeedback therapy called *Freeze-Framer*® to train individuals to generate a state of positive emotions. The computer program uses a finger or earlobe sensor to read the HRV, with the screen displaying the subject's emotional state in real time. The user is encouraged to focus on the area around the heart, where people subjectively feel love, care and appreciation. These mind-sets have been shown to help balance the nervous systems. While engaged in the Freeze-Frame® process, the heart rhythms become smooth and coherent, affecting the perceptual centers in the brain. This initiates a more balanced perspective.

The Benefits of Freeze-Framer® Biofeedback

The reported benefits include reduced stress, increased energy and resilience, increased efficiency, enhanced athletic performance, improved test-taking skill, greater mental clarity for decision-making and creativity, enhanced emotional balance, and improved listening ability.

In 2004 The Institute of HeartMath introduced a new learning program designed to help students excel in learning and test taking. This interactive CD-ROM, known as the TestEdge®, "is an engaging multimedia course that teaches students scientifically validated tools and strategies to overcome test anxiety, discouragement, and indifference, while boosting focus, motivation, and clarity."[29] Used in over 200 American schools, it is now being funded by a one million dollar evaluation by the US Department of Education. See this book's web site for a link to this resource.

On the corporate front, this company provides such biofeedback programs as Executive Freeze-Framer® Interactive Learning System.

Emotional Freedom Technique (EFT)

According to the *State Dependent Memory Learning and Behavior* theory, events are encoded in a person's physiology on a cellular/molecular level. These events include both the memory and the emotion attached to it. They reside in energy fields that flow on unique major neural pathways, corresponding to what some people call meridians.

Dr. Pert, mentioned earlier, states that our thoughts convert to emotions that in turn become neuropeptides. The neuropeptides, which are strings of amino acids, communicate with the body on the biochemical level.[30]

This whole concept was extremely well explained in the movie *What The Bleep Do We Know*. Many people have seen it over and over again to gain a deeper understanding. Dr. Dõv Baron of Vancouver, Canada, has an insightful paper of his impressions of the movie. Check out this book's web site for a link.

EFT is one of the many techniques in the new field of *Energy Psychology*. It is in the branch known as *meridian therapies*. The technique removes negative emotions, reduces or eliminates pain, releases phobias, and assists in setting and implementing positive goals. EFT is a form of psychological acupressure, based on the same energy meridians used in traditional acupuncture, to treat emotional disorders. Focusing on the issue and stimulating the major neural pathways initiates a memory process causing change by unblocking the emotional short-circuit. This process results in substituting positive emotions for the negative emotions, which were previously learned and associated with the issue.

The process initially requires the person to think about the event or issue. Simple tapping with the fingertips is used to input kinetic energy onto specific meridians on the hand, head, and chest. This combination of tapping the energy meridians and voicing specific phrases works to clear the emotional block from the body's bio-energetic system. This restores the mind and body's balance, which is essential for optimal learning and mental health. EFT can dramatically enhance intellectual performance simply by eliminating the emotional lids on our intellectual potential. See this book's web site for a link to this resource.

Some of the other energy therapies are Matrix Works, Break Set Free Fast, Energy Diagnostic & Treatment Method, Attractor Field Therapy, Thought Energy Synchronization, Acu-Power, Healing From the Body Level Up, Neuro-Emotional Technique, Tapas Acupressure Technique, Psychological Kinesiology, and Healing Touch.

TimeLine Therapy™ Techniques

The Unconscious Mind believes that it protects by suppressing memories that have unresolved negative emotions. These stored emotions block the natural flow of energy and information through the neural pathways. The result can be damage to the body, mind, and spirit.

I believe that each of us is where we are today psychologically because of conscious and unconscious decisions that we have made throughout our life. Tad James, PhD designed TimeLine Therapy techniques to help people eradicate the negative emotions and limiting decisions that prevent them from experiencing a full and joyful life. The TimeLine Therapy experience reveals information and solutions in order to prepare us for future challenges.

> *A vital part of letting go of negative emotions is learning what we need to learn from them.*
>
> Dr. Tad James, Developer of
> TimeLine Therapy™ Technique

To effectively let go of a negative emotion, it is necessary to release every occurrence of that emotion since it was first experienced. Releasing emotion from just a single event will not necessarily produce a complete recovery. The TimeLine Therapy procedure is specific and structured. Although appearing to be done in a conscious state, it can bring about a light trance.

- The first step is to ask the subject to visualize and declare the track of his or her own timeline. This is a person's perception of how time is organized in his or her own mind. The past is in one direction and the future is in another. The timeline may run through a person's head or appear out in front. It may be straight-lined or curved. It may be vertical, horizontal, or inclined. It may be any size, color, or texture. It may be smooth or irregular.

- The second step is to ask the subject to imagine rising above the timeline. The subject is then invited to imagine traveling back above the timeline to find a time before the specific negative emotion or limiting decision was first experienced. The key here is for the subject to **feel** the emotional state that was present **before** that *initial sensitizing event*. There are a number of detailed procedures that occur at this point that I will not include in this short description.

- The third step is to ask the subject to return to "now," and, on the way, to clear away any and all episodes of this specific negative emotion or self-limiting decision.

A complete round (all three steps) is achieved for each emotion or decision. Releasing negative emotions must be achieved in a specific order: anger, sadness, fear, and guilt, etc. Once the negative emotions are cleared, the subject is better able to handle stress and has clearer thinking, and is now in a position to insert goals at specific points in the future arm of the timeline. (See chapter 3 on Goal-setting.)

I received my TimeLine Therapy training and most of my NLP training from Advanced Neuro Dynamics. Aside from providing audio, video, and books, this company conducts live courses in North America and Australia. See www.UnleashingBook.com for a link to this resource.

The Science of Mind-Kinetics®

In the introduction to this book, I outlined many potential obstructions to your learning. Coaching and Leadership International (CLI), has researched this subject extensively. Their list is called *Causes of Unclarity*. You can find it in appendix 6.

What are the consequences of Unclarity? In simply terms, your body, mind, spirit, and emotions do not work at their full capacity. Subconscious patterns emerge, such as muddled thinking, negative self-talk, unproductive behaviors, and poor interpersonal skills. CLI calls this "living in *Lower Power*," and this is seen in seven distinct areas of life: career, financial, family, social, spiritual, intellectual, and physical.

To help people to move to their *Higher Power*, a frame of mind where their emotional charges are eliminated and they are clear on solutions to their issues, CLI has created tools called Power Coaching® with Mind-Kinetics® or PCMK™. The Science of Mind-Kinetics® is defined as "the science which opens the mind and empowers the client to receive new ideas and take action for permanent positive change." These tools are available in a self-coaching form, as well as with the assistance of one of their certified practitioners.

Great success has been experienced with clients who have such emotional problems as drug addiction, bedwetting, and dysfunctional family relationships. In the corporate sphere, whole corporate teams are now working harmoniously together, and workplace harassment and abuse have diminished. The Brain Walk® was introduced earlier in this book as a way for you to better integrate the information. It is an integral component of PCMK™. Executives who faithfully do The Brain Walk® every day make better decisions faster. What follows is a brief overview of the key components on which the tools are based.

Physiological/Biological Shift

In Chapter 2, I outlined how our brain learns. Earlier in this chapter, I discussed the ground-breaking work on emotions by Dr. Candace Pert. The science behind how emotions establish physiological patterns in the brain is incontrovertible. Just as our eyes and ears are "receptors" of incoming data, on a micro level there are cellular receptors, and we have millions of them. Once a pattern is ingrained by the reinforcing of habits, it takes specific interventions to release them. These tools let loose or "pop" the cellular receptors in order to release emotions and memories. Relieved from this "stuckness" in Lower Power, the client's receptors allow a new flow of oxygen and glucose to the thinking cells. With nourished cells, the client is able to think more clearly. Solutions to problems and challenges are now more readily available.

Image-Streaming

Innovation is not the product of logical thought, even though the final product is tied to a logical structure.

Albert Einstein

Whenever Einstein had a problem or a challenge, he invited his right hemisphere to provide the answers. He would plant a specific problem or challenge firmly in his brain, then pick up his violin and play. Apparently, he would not stop playing until he received answers from his innovative right brain.

The second method he employed was the "rock" method. Einstein would sit in a chair, hands on his knees and a rock in each hand. Once again, he would firmly plant a specific challenge in his brain. He would tell his left brain to shut off, and his right brain to turn on. He would sit patiently waiting for his right brain to give him solutions in the form of images, feelings, memory pictures, sense experiences, and muscular sensations – all pieces of what he called "combinatory play." From time to time the rocks would fall and hit his toe. This was his clue that he had fallen asleep! He would wake up and start the image-streaming process all over again.

Einstein was a master at *image streaming* – streaming in solutions to problems and challenges from his **right brain**. Having received the images and feelings from his right brain, Einstein would then use his logical **left brain** to decode the messages to determine how this representation was a solution to his challenge.

Einstein is not the only genius to have mastered the art of image-streaming. The greatest thinkers of all time – including Plato, Confucius, da Vinci, Emerson, Gandhi, and Socrates – had mastered this same art.

PCMK™ tools use image-streaming as one of many methods to re-train the brain to think like a genius. Image-streaming was used to create many of these tools.

Bilateral Thinking

Bilateral thinking is the ability to switch easily between left and right hemispheres. These tools have been scientifically engineered with questions that stimulate movement between left and right hemispheres, eventually creating a bilateral thinker of the user. Those who master bilateral thinking, master their lives.

Whole-Brain Thinking

Much of this book deals with unconscious processing.

The PCMK™ tools generate bilateral brain activity and, concurrently, interaction between the conscious and sub-conscious minds.

> *It is our unconscious which holds the power of a Leonardo da Vinci or an Einstein.*
>
> Dr. Win Wenger, Author:
> *The Einstein Factor*

> *When a person has access to the intuitive–creative–visual right–brain and the analytical–logical–verbal left–brain, then the whole brain is working.*
>
> Stephen Covey Author:
> *The 7 Habits of Highly Successful People*

Color

A consultant was asked to come to a school to find out why a specific classroom was causing discipline problems. It didn't matter which students were there or, indeed, what teacher was conducting the lesson. This particular room was jinxed, and no one knew why. The consultant walked into the room and within three seconds said, "Change the carpet." It was mainly red. Once the carpet had been replaced, the discipline problems evaporated. If you're a teacher, trainer, or just expect to give a presentation sometime, take a look at what I write about the color red in Chapter 10.

Color detection is part of our innate survival makeup. Since our mind responds to color stimuli, The Brain Walk® map incorporates it for that very reason. The colors have been carefully chosen to create a physiological shift in the brain.

The Universal Laws of Human Behavior

If you align yourself with these principles, you will find that the quality of your life will improve in direct relation to the degree to which you embrace them. You will experience a greater sense of belonging and purpose. Relationships will be stable on both the personal and business front.

The universal laws are unbreakable, unchangeable principles of life that operate inevitably, in all phases of our lives and existence, for all human beings and all things, everywhere, all the time. Here is a synopsis of just a few of these laws.

- **Law of Service:** The more I love myself, the more I can love/serve others.

- **Law of Equality:** I am just as important as the next person. Therefore, my true needs, wants, desires, hopes, and dreams and their fulfillment are as important as those of any other soul in existence.

- **Law of Choice:** If I want to change my life, I must change my choices.

- **Law of Belief:** What I think, both consciously and unconsciously, I become. My thoughts are my actions. I must turn negative words, thoughts, and actions into positive ones.

- **First Law of Increase:** What I resist, persists. My negative patterns repeat themselves until I choose to break through them.

- **Law of Attraction:** I attract people, places, and things into my life. The point is to create your own life through attracting what you want. (See this book's web site for a link to the Law of Attraction Book site)

- **Law of Cause and Effect:** What I sow, I reap.

A basic understanding of these laws of human behavior moves us from the realm of blaming self and others, towards a place of being able to live in harmony with others. Just a discussion of these laws can raise our consciousness on an issue.

The Values of Humanity

With your experience of The Brain Walk®, you will have used the random generator to present a 'value' that symbolizes a stressor or challenge in your life. Have you noticed how The Brain Walk® has been able to help you in becoming more aware of challenges in your conscious and unconscious? A powerful component of The Brain Walk® is the use of values, which touch the very depth of our being.

When a value is presented, such as respect, honesty, acceptance, or self-love, the process asks you to think about what is stressing or challenging you about that value, at that moment in time. All of us possess the seventy-five main values of humanity, and each of us chooses which values to exhibit. For example, some people are honest while others prefer not to be. Some individuals respect the feelings of others, while some choose to use power and control to de-spirit others.

PCMK™ tools use these seventy-five main values of humanity to inspire thought, and to bring out the unconscious reasons for our inability to be as successful as we would like to be. Next, we "pop" our cellular receptors for clarity, solutions, and permanent positive change.

Strategies

The tools have been developed to allow all users to go wild using their imagination and to tap into the highest creative centers of their brain for innovative solutions to everything in life.

These quick and easy tools teach us that innovation is not the product of logical thought, but rather the product of mastering whole-brain thinking. Daily practice with these tools can provide you with the structure with which to do so.

If you would like to learn more about the self-coaching tools, find a certified practitioner, or become one yourself... check out this book's website for a link to Coaching and Leadership International.

> *Logic will get you from*
> *A to B;*
> *imagination will take you*
> *everywhere.*
>
> Albert Einstein

1   What is your greatest learning from this chapter?

2. Who in your life brings up strong "negative" feelings for you, such as anger, frustration, or sadness?

3. CALL TO ACTION:
    Visit www.UnleashingBook.com to link to the CLI site. Choose the free self-coaching tool entitled "The Brain Walk® – A Journey for Peace of Mind." This tool will assist you in becoming clearer on how you can release some of these intense feelings and become more peaceful about the relationship in question.

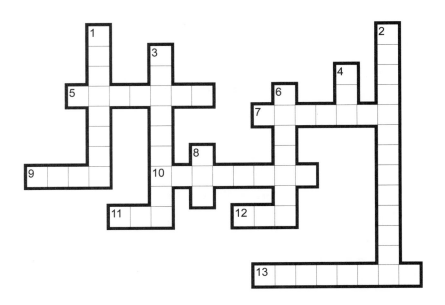

ACROSS	**DOWN**
5. A condition of traumatized children	1. The right kind of emotion acts as a _____ to learning
7. Learned helplessness is _____-specific	2. Built–in human defense mechanisms
9. IQ measures the _____ –brain intelligences only	3. Neural pathways are developed and reinforced by the degree they are _____
10. Emotions are primary and universal _____ tools	4. Number of emotions a person can have at one time
11. A common problem in the short days of winter	6. Negative emotions can lay _____ for years
12. A form of psychological acupressure	8. Beat–to–beat changes in heart rhythm patterns
13. Emotions receive neurological message _____	

BRILLIANT NOTES

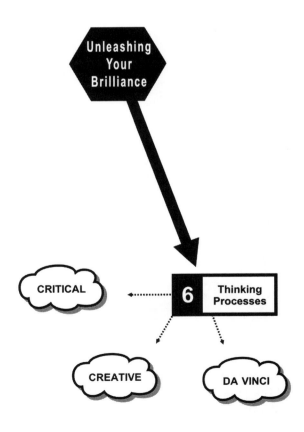

Your Thinking Processes

*It sounded an excellent plan,
no doubt, and very neatly and
simply arranged.*

*The only difficulty was,
she had not the smallest idea
how to set about it.*

Lewis Carroll,
of Alice in *Alice in Wonderland*

**In order for you to acquire and process information, you
need essential learning and thinking skills. This chapter will
explore how to increase your creative and critical thinking
capacities through instruction and practice.**

Most students do not score well on tests that measure ability
to recognize assumptions, evaluate arguments, and appraise
inferences. In order to function successfully in a highly technical
and rapidly changing world, thinking skills are crucial. These
skills are more than techniques; they typify a general attitude
of mind. Teaching children to become effective thinkers is
increasingly recognized as an immediate goal of education.

There is a misconception that creative thinking and critical thinking are opposites. Actually, they are complementary, and by skillfully employing both, you can boost the quality of your communication and learning. You can approach this in two ways. Firstly, there is whole-brain stimulation, as outlined in Chapter 8. Secondly, familiarize yourself with the Basic Rest Activity Cycle that was explained in Chapter 2. The active period of the cycle is typified by greater activity in the logical left brain. The rest period of the cycle shows more neural firing in the creative right brain. If you are composing an email, a letter, a speech, or any other form of communication, write it out, and put it away for about twenty-five to forty-five minutes. When you review it, your perceptions will be much different. If you were in the creative cycle, you can now scrutinize it with a critical eye, and vice-versa.

Critical Thinking

From kindergarten to graduate school, our entire education system is designed to teach people how to memorize information. Students are usually rewarded for regurgitation, not comprehension. They are trained **what** to think, not **how** to think.

Critical thinking is used to make rational decisions and solve problems. It uses a process of determining the authenticity, accuracy, or value of something. It is characterized by the ability to seek reasons and alternatives, perceive the total situation, and draw upon known facts and principles so as to arrive at a conclusion, and to be prepared to change one's view based upon the evidence. This narrowing-down activity is also known as vertical thinking, logical thinking, or analytical thinking. It is sequential and must be correct at each and every step in order to proceed. Evidence in this type of thinking must be obtained through observation, evaluation, comparing and contrasting, prioritizing, classifying, summarizing, sequencing, predicting, inferring, synthesizing, and determining cause and effect in a fixed fashion. Being rigid, the thinking follows the most-likely path to reach the most-likely solution. Once the supposed resolution is reached, thinking stops.

One simple example of this is in interpreting the questions on a True/False test paper. Critical thinking would show that, generally speaking, the words *always* or *never*, indicate a false statement. Those appearing with words like *usually, sometimes,* or *often*, are frequently true statements.

Decision-Making

The process for making decisions often begins with making assumptions about the problem at hand, the events as observed, and the implications interpreted on many levels. Facts are scrutinized to ensure that they are not actually beliefs. Consideration is then given as to whether the depth and breadth of the information is appropriate. The stream of thought can blindly follow the course set, even if the assumptions and impressions are false. Naturally, erroneous assumptions lead to incorrect conclusions. The process then takes into account arguments for and against a position. The final step is the challenging of the conclusion, which may lead to a better outcome.

Problem-Solving

Solving problems is a process that begins with developing a clear unambiguous grasp of the dilemma. The next step is to generate a host of alternatives with a "systems thinking" approach. This means considering the problem, not in isolation, but in terms of how it may impact the whole. Questioning will provide a clear definition of the problem and will help identify the goal. The creative thinking skills then come into play by generating alternatives. These are narrowed down, and the consequences of the remaining alternatives are considered. Acting upon the chosen solution follows.

The more we experience,
the more we become,
the better we problem—solve.

Bertice Berry, PhD, speaker and author,
I'm on My Way, but Your Foot Is on My Head

It is the mark of an educated mind
to be able to entertain a thought
without accepting it.

Aristotle

Most of us look at problems and attempt to find immediate solutions. That's what the analytical process entails. By getting analytical too quickly, we forfeit the likelihood for an even more creative solution.

Creative Thinking

> *We are more than a sum of our knowledge;*
> *we are products of our imagination.*
>
> ... Ancient Proverb

Creative thinking encompasses a novel way of seeing or doing things that is characterized by four components:

- *Fluency*, or generating many alternatives.

- *Flexibility*, or shifting perspective easily and restructuring patterns.

- *Originality*, or conceiving of something new.

- *Elaboration*, or building on other ideas.

It takes what we already know and combines it into new relationships, resulting in new images, ideas, or solutions. This expanding activity is also known as *lateral thinking*. Edward de Bono, founder and director of the Cognitive Research Trust at Cambridge University in the UK, recommends that children should begin their training in lateral thinking at about the age of seven.

> *Creativity requires the courage to let go of certainties.*
>
> Social psychologist Erich Fromm

Creative thinking skills use very different approaches than those employed in critical thinking.

Creativity can be described as letting go of certainties.

Gail Sheehy Author of
the *Passages* series

Creativity is often less ordered, structured, or predictable, and it involves a much more relaxed, open, playful style. This can require some risk-taking.

I like nonsense; it wakes up the brain cells. Fantasy is a necessary ingredient in living, it's a way of looking at life through the wrong end of a telescope. Which is what I do, and that enables you to laugh at life's realities.

Dr. Seuss, the alter ego of
Theodor Seuss Geisel (1904–1991)

The objective of creative thinking is not just to uncover a single right answer, but, rather, to allow numerous possibilities to surface, regardless of whether or not they seem correct. This can be difficult if you're more analytical and logical. You might even think that this is risky, because of the possibility of making a mistake or not coming up with any answer at all.

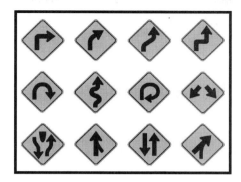

> *To live a creative life, we must lose our fear of being wrong.*
>
> Joseph Chilton Pearce, author of
> *The Crack in the Cosmic Egg* among others

In order to facilitate creative thinking, strong emotional self-management is often needed. You have to be prepared to cope with risk, confusion, disorder, and frustration.

The Creative Thinking Process

Creative thinking skills involve looking for many possible answers rather than just one. We need to be set to make mistakes in order to learn what worked well and what didn't.

> *Anyone who has never made a mistake has never tried anything new.*
>
> Albert Einstein

- Allow the flow of wild and crazy suggestions, without any criticism.

- Treat all ideas as if they may contain the seeds of something potentially useful.

- Practice free-form activities such as doodling, daydreaming, playing with a theory or suggestion, brainstorming, and storyboarding.

- Ask the same question at least twenty times and give a different answer each time.

- Combine some of the features of two different objects or ideas.

- Substitute people, resources, or places.

- Magnify or minimize the frequency, size, or resources.

- Eliminate, condense, omit, streamline.

- Rearrange or reverse layout, sequence, roles, pace, habitual perspectives and routines.

- Polarize two competing viewpoints by expanding them to ridiculous extremes.

Our task, regarding creativity, is to help children climb their own mountains, as high as possible.

Education specialist
Loris Malaguzzi

Random Word-Association Brainstorming

When I was first exposed to this method, I was somewhat skeptical. The occasion was a brainstorming evening to generate new ideas for this book's title. As our group gathered, Anne, a hypnotherapist colleague of mine, suggested this innovative brainstorming approach.

With the topic identified beforehand, the process began with a member of the group being asked to open a dictionary to any page. He then randomly selected a common noun, which was written on a flip chart. Each person was asked for a single word that he or she associated with that noun. The group was then asked to suggest associations between each of these words and the topic, accelerated learning. The words flowed in amazing quantity. We repeated this process a few times.

Why did this technique work so well? It's really quite simple. In a typical brainstorming session, when members of a group are asked to come up with ideas or solutions to a problem, their minds access their memory banks and download what is already known about the issue. Introducing the random word method forces the mind to find a link between dissimilar things. Because of the gap between the random word and the topic, ideas may be quite unusual, or even off the wall. As the group members build on each others' ideas, they generate more creative solutions.

This method is fast and simple, and usually leads to ideas that are more creative than those generated from the classic brainstorming format. See Appendix 5 for another real-life example that took place when a telephone company had their group focus on the issue of how to increase revenue from their pay phones.

Six Thinking Hats

Often while discussing ideas, projects, or new directions, people assume argumentative positions, and as a result, nothing productive comes about. Six Thinking Hats is an effective creative thinking system developed by Edward de Bono. Easily applied, it enhances creativity, innovation, and productivity This structured approach fosters collaboration among diverse participants with divergent perspectives in many disciplines and at many levels.

Six Thinking Hats teaches how to separate thinking into six distinct modes. Each mode is identified with its own metaphorical "hat." By mentally wearing and switching "hats", a person changes the mode of thinking. This tactic enables a group to move towards constructive dialogue as everyone wears the same color hat at the same time and takes on the role linked with that color hat. The result is that several perspectives are evaluated and a fruitful conclusion is reached. This takes brainstorming to a new level.

- The Blue Hat is used to manage the thinking process and is usually employed by the chairperson of the meeting.

- The White Hat calls for information known or needed.

- The Yellow Hat symbolizes values and benefits and why something may work.

- The Black Hat is judgment – the devil's advocate or why something may not work.

- The Red Hat signifies feelings, hunches, and intuition.

- The Green Hat focuses on creativity: possibilities, alternatives, and new ideas.

Apart from its educational value for creativity training, the tool shines in the corporate world in such areas as meeting facilitation, meeting management, team productivity, communication, program development, process improvement, project management, problem-solving, and decision-making. As mentioned earlier, creative processes enable critical and analytical thinking.

Leonardo da Vinci – A Whole-Brain Thinker

In NLP, we talk about modeling. In his excellent book, *How to Think Like Leonardo da Vinci*, Michael Gelb suggests that the genius traits of da Vinci can be modeled with the following seven steps.

- *Curiosità:* An insatiably curious approach to life and an unrelenting quest for continuous learning.

- *Dimonstrazione:* A commitment to test knowledge through experience, persistence, and a willingness to learn from mistakes.

- *Sensazione:* The continual refinement of the senses, especially sight, as a means to enliven experience.

- *Sfumato:* A willingness to embrace ambiguity, paradox and uncertainty.

- *Arte/Scienza:* the development of the balance between science and art, logic and imagination – whole-brain thinking.

- *Corporalita:* The cultivation of grace, ambidexterity, fitness and poise.

- *Connessione:* a recognition of and appreciation for the interconnectedness of all things and phenomena – Systems thinking.

Compare this list with the Four Links of Effective Learning in Chapter 3.

Meta-cognition is the awareness and control of your own thinking. In this chapter, we have examined the two interdependent parts of thinking.

- Critical thinking is the reasonable, reflective thinking that is focused on distinguishing between your current reality and your desired outcome. You acknowledge your own biases, with an objective and logical approach.

- Creative thinking is your ability to form new combinations of ideas to satisfy your goals.

> *There's a saying among prospectors:*
> *Go out looking for one thing,*
> *and that's all you'll ever find.*
>
> Cinematographer
> Robert Flaherty

1 **What is your greatest learning from this chapter?**

2. **What would you like to change about the way that you think?**

3. **CALL TO ACTION:**
    Visit www.UnleashingBook.com to link to the CLI site. Choose the free self-coaching tool entitled "Life Review." This tool invites you to study all seven areas of your life and articulate the many obstacles you have overcome in each area of life. Take a moment to celebrate how you are already a great thinker.

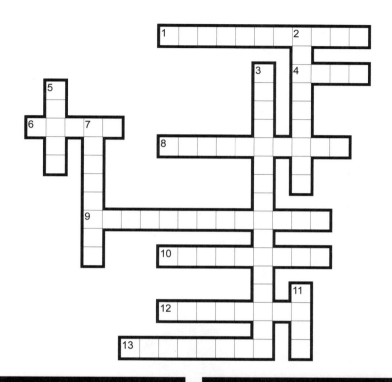

ACROSS

1. The process for making decisions begins with making _____ of the problem
4. Usually, sometimes, or often, are frequently _____ statements
6. _____ Hat is the devil's advocate
8. The Green Hat focuses on _____
9. Six Thinking Hats fosters _____
10. There is a misconception that creative thinking and critical thinking are _____
12. Education systems teach people how to _____ ...

ACROSS

information
13. By mentally wearing and switching "hats", a person changes the mode of _____

DOWN

2. The Red Hat signifies feelings, hunches and _____
3. Narrowing–down activity
5. Always or never, indicate a _____ statement
7. _____ thinking is used to make rational decisions
11. Creativity is _____ predictable than critical thinking

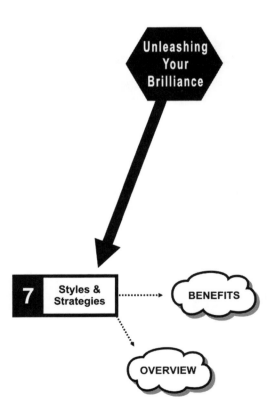

PERSONALITY STYLES & LEARNING STRATEGIES

In this chapter we will learn how it is possible to identify people's preferences, in order to recognize their natural strengths and weaknesses for a given set of circumstances. *Learning strategies* **are how people select, acquire, organize, interact, internalize, and process new and challenging material.**

> *Because of the infinite variation in the way individuals are assembled, it must be assumed that the sentient properties of any one person, like his or her fingerprints, could never be identical with those of another.*
>
> *It is probable, therefore, that there does not exist or ever will exist one person exactly like another.*
>
> Paul McLean,
> *The Triune Brain in Evolution*

The words of the language,
as written and spoken,
do not seem to play any role in my
mechanisms of thought.

Albert Einstein

Individuals each have their own unique ways of mastering new and difficult subject matter. As people grow and learn, they expand their ability to operate successfully in unfamiliar environments. Some of these skill and knowledge areas become more highly developed than others. No one is served by simply labeling individuals according to their apparent learning abilities and behaviors.

Benefits of Knowing One's Learning Style

Learning about our own personality type helps us to understand why certain areas in life come easily to us, while others are more of a struggle. Knowing one's type or style is an indication of how one takes in and incorporates information. Discovering other people's personality types helps us to understand the most effective way to communicate with them, and how they function best. The practice of classifying by personality types or styles maintains that each of us has a natural preference that falls into one or more categories. Our native personality type indicates how we are likely to deal with different situations that life presents, and in which environments we are most comfortable. (See Chapter 5 on *Emotions and Learning*) Usually, individuals are a blend of all categories to one degree or another, and can change their style over time.

It is critical for teachers and educational administrators to appreciate that a conflict in styles between teachers and students inhibits excellence in learning.[31]

> *Each person's map of the world is as unique as their thumbprint. There are no two people alike; no two people who understand the same sentence the same way.*
>
> Hypnotherapist
> Milton H. Erickson MD

An alert teacher can defuse these conflicts by balancing structured and unstructured activities through both inductive and deductive course material.

INDUCTIVE

From specific observations, thus finding patterns to form general conclusions.

DEDUCTIVE

From general to specific.

In order to reach all students, presentations must appeal to Visual, Auditory, and Kinesthetic learners. (See Chapter 10 on NLP.) Weight should also be given to the learning environment, and to the students' beliefs, attitudes, and motivations. This wide set of variables can be overwhelming; a lot of the responsibility of learning must be conveyed to the student. As teachers begin to appreciate that their unique instructional styles are appropriate for only a limited number of students, they may become more willing to offer a greater variety of teaching methods.

Overview of Various Learning Styles

In other chapters of this book, we examine multiple intelligences, dominance factors, and the NLP representational systems. Please remember that the identification of a learner's traits is used as a general indication of how that person takes in and puts together information, and by no means completely defines the person.

There are literally dozens of formal classification systems that put learners into defined boxes. Some of these are The Five Factor Model, 4-Mat, Myers-Briggs Type Indicator, and DiSC®.

Here are examples of the many styles and categories used by some classification systems:

orderliness, adventurousness, helpfulness, image focus, hypersensitivity, detachment, caution, strength, calmness, considerate learner, analytic learner, dynamic learner, inventive learner, openness to experience, intellect, conscientiousness, extraversion, agreeableness, religiosity, honesty, deceptiveness, conservativeness, conceit, thrift, humorousness, sensuality, masculinity–femininity, common sense learners, dynamic learners, perceiving, processing, innovative learners, analytic learners, emotional stability.

What follows are two of the most popular systems.

The Myers-Briggs Type Indicator

The Myers-Briggs Type Indicator is the most popular personality tool in the world. It is based on the findings of Swiss psychologist/anthropologist Carl Jung and has over forty years of research and development to support it. The Myers-Briggs Type Indicator reflects the concept that people express traits along the four ranges shown below. The possible combinations of the basic preferences form sixteen different personality types. It is the core of the basic Meta programs of Neurolinguistic Programming.

- **Gaining Energy:** *Extroversion* (focusing on the outside world and getting energy by interacting with people and doing things) versus *Introversion* (focusing on the inner world and getting energy through reflecting on information, ideas and/or concepts).

- **Gathering Information:** *Sensing* (perceiving and trusting facts, details, and present realities) versus *Intuition* (attending to and trusting interrelationships, theories and future possibilities).

- **Making Decisions:** *Thinking* (making decisions using logical, objective analysis) versus *Feeling* (making decisions to create harmony by applying person-centered values).

- **Dealing with the World:** *Judging* (organized, orderly and decisive) versus *Perceiving* (flexible, adaptable and like to keep options open).

If you wish to take an online Myers-Briggs test, see the link at www.UnleashingBook.com

DiSC® Classic

Each human has a unique view of how he or she fits into the world. We see our environment as either favorable or unfavorable. We see ourselves as being either more or less powerful than that environment. When faced with identical stimuli, each of us has a distinctive emotional response, and this individual behavior can be measured. DiSC® Classic is a tool designed to explore current behavioral characteristics in four areas: *dominance, influence, steadiness*, and *conscientiousness*. Hence the acronym DiSC®.

After completing a short written or online questionnaire, the results will indicate corresponding tendencies, needs, preferred environments, and effective strategies for each. The combination of scores in these four dimensions may indicate one of fifteen classic profiles. An individual's scores may be altered over time due to a change in coping skills and a perception of their environment.

You can discover your DiSC® profile by linking from www.UnleashingBook.com A moderate fee will be charged. If you choose to do this, I would like to give you some advice to optimize your experience.

- Consider the context before you begin to answer the questions. You may behave one way at work, and a different way at home. Determine your focus (parent, manager, leader, etc.), then answer the questions about how you behave in that context.

- Once you have completed the questionnaire, you will receive your feedback by email. If you are under a great deal of chaos in your life, your score will reflect that. Your results will indicate strengths and weaknesses in a number of areas of your life, and offer suggestions on how you might consider altering your behavior.

- If you wish to do some personal growth work, do The Brain Walk® on the specific feedback that you receive. This tool will assist you in developing innovative solutions for any unproductive behaviors. You can measure your success by taking the DiSC® again six to twelve months later, or by asking friends and family if they have observed any changes in your personality over a similar time frame.

Recognition of Learning Styles Leads to Development of Strategies

As early as 1956, educators began to consider the mental processing behavior of individuals engaged in problem-solving. Since the 1970s there has been a progressive shift away from a mechanistic model of human learning (automatic and scientific) to a model where learners can **proactively organize their body of knowledge to create their own reality**. This is the essence of assertive learning. Teachers and trainers who support this approach end up with motivated learners.

The purpose of this chapter was to give you a greater understanding of how we all learn differently. These tools can assist you in planning your learning strategies, resulting in personal, professional, or academic excellence.

1. What is your greatest learning from this chapter?

BRILLIANT NOTES

_____

_____

_____

_____

_____

_____

_____

_____

_____

_____

_____

_____

_____

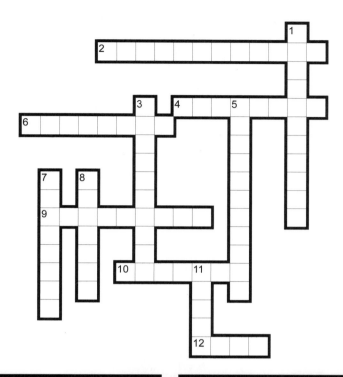

2. Focusing on the inner world

4. Who said "Each person's map of the world is as unique as their thumbprint"

6. The Myers–Briggs Type Indicator is based on the findings of this Swiss psychologist/anthropologist.

9. From general to specific

10. Conflict in styles between teachers and students _____ excellence in learning

12. This explores behavioral characteristics in four areas: dominance, influence, steadiness, and conscientiousness.

1. Native personality type indicates in which environments we are most _____

3. Identification of a learner's traits is used as a general _____ of how that person takes in and integrates information

5. Discovering other people's personality types helps us to _____ with them

7. Presentations must appeal to visual, _____, and kinesthetic learners

8. MBTI – organized, orderly and decisive

11. Usually, individuals are a _____ of all categories

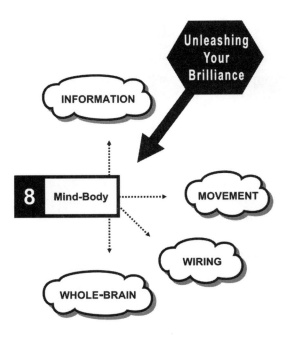

THE INTRIGUING MIND-BODY UNITY

The vast majority of information for this section has been gleaned from Dr. Carla Hannaford's books:

> *Smart Moves: Why Learning is Not All in Your Head* and *The Dominance Factor.*

> Thank you to Great River Books of Salt Lake City, UT, USA

> Additional information was provided by Kim Barthel, OTR, author of *Evidence and Art: Merging Forces in Pediatric Therapy.*

> *The human body is...*
> *the place that memories call home.*
> Dr. Deepak Chopra

The study of body language, physical exercise, anatomy, and physiology is called *Kinesiology*. In terms of the brain-body connection, we consider emotions, and feelings such as the "gut reaction." This chapter explores the significant influence of movement on the learning process.

Tell me and I forget;
show me and I remember;
involve me and I understand.

Anonymous

Your thoughts, learning, intelligence, and creativity are processed, not solely by the brain, but also by the whole physical body working in concert with the mind. In the early 1990s, neuroscientists discovered that the areas in the brain related to muscle movement – the basal ganglia and the cerebellum – are also essential in synchronizing thought. These areas are connected to the frontal lobe area, where the planning of the order and timing of future events transpires.[32] Muscular activities, particularly coordinated movements, appear to stimulate the production of *neurotrophins*. These natural substances stimulate growth of nerve cells and increase the number of neural connections in the brain, especially between the two hemispheres.[33]

The more the brain is challenged, the better it performs. Athletes and actors have always known this. Even imagery changes patterns in the brain.[34] Obviously, the more vivid the image, the greater the chance of successful completion.

Put this into the context of goal-setting. Like any muscle, **the brain craves exercise to ensure growth and health.** Before we take a look at how activity helps a person to learn, I'd like to share with you some of the fascinating features of the neural and vestibular systems.

In Chapter 4, we examined kinesthetic intelligence, and later, in Chapter 10, we will discuss the kinesthetic learning style.

How Information Flows Through Your Body

Neurons are nerve cells that are adapted specifically for transmission of electrical messages throughout the body. They come in three functional forms.

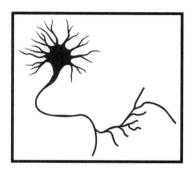

- *Sensory neurons* carry information to the central nervous system (brain and spinal cord) from the proprioceptors, eyes, ears, skin, tongue, and nose. Proprioceptors are sense organs that relay information about muscle position, tension, equilibrium, and the activity of joints. They are located in the muscles, tendons, joints, and the inner ear.

- *Motor neurons* carry out orders from the central nervous system by animating the muscles and glands.

- *Intermediate (Association) neurons* account for almost 100 percent of the neurons in the central nervous system . They are responsible for relaying data throughout the central nervous system and specifically to the motor neurons.

The neurons in a newborn's brain are only slightly organized, and are primed to begin the process of learning. A newborn responds to light, sounds, and gravity. The only fears with which it is born are of heights and loud noises; all the rest are learned.

Survival drives much of the infant's learning, so its priorities are food, warmth, and shelter. This survival instinct continues to have influence, albeit diminishing, throughout a lifetime of learning. As the infant begins to physically interact with its environment, communications between the neurons cause short branching fibers known as *dendrites* to begin to grow and extend *spiny protuberances*. Throughout life, dendrites will grow in response to stimulation, and shrink under adverse conditions. The inherent plasticity of the human brain is immense. Given the proper amount of hydration, nutrition, oxygen, stimulation, and freedom to move, the mind will learn at a fantastic rate. It is later, when students are corralled into classroom rows that the learning curves begin to lose their early dramatic climb.

Back in the 1960s and 1970s, open education practices allowed freedom of movement for students. Although these approaches are currently out of style, some schools still operate hybrid environments where elements of the student-centered models are judiciously combined with a more-disciplined environment. The teachers and principals who support these concepts keep a low profile.

Progressive corporate trainers are increasingly being trained in accelerated learning techniques to create stimulating programs. A greater number of executives are beginning to understand that an effective presentation requires more than colorful slides. They are now including creative interactive elements.

As an independent learner, you have full control over how you study. Design your study activities to include motion. Later in this chapter, I will give you some ideas.

Your Sense of Movement and Balance

The *vestibular system* and the *proprioceptor system* cooperate to provide an awareness of the exact position of a person's body.

The vestibular system contributes to the sense of movement and balance, and maintains both *static equilibrium* (body orientation when standing still) and *dynamic equilibrium* (body position relative to acceleration, deceleration and rotation). It is central to everything we do.

As we experience and explore our physical environment, we take in new information through our senses and new sensory patterns are built into intricate neural networks. This sensory system is so crucial to learning that it begins maturing a couple of months after conception. By the fifth month in utero, the vestibular system is almost fully developed. Reports of movement and position from the inner ear merge with information from the eyes and are conducted to the *Reticular Activating System* (RAS), located at the base of the brain. This small acorn-like system is the filer and integrator of our ability to analyze movement. All of our experience, and therefore learning, involves the sensory-motor systems.

> *All truly great thoughts are conceived by walking.*
>
> Friedrich Wilheim Nietzsche

When I was an undergrad, I was faced with two challenges. I had no aptitude for accounting and I disliked writing essays. I had to do something. Although this was before I knew anything about hypnosis, I did know about affirmations. My exercise regime included a daily one-hour walk, so, as I walked, I simply exclaimed out loud, "I love accounting and I excel at accounting." My other affirmation was, "I love writing essays and I excel at writing essays." Guess what – After a few months I landed an "A–" in accounting, and my essay writing began to flow.

How Movement Energizes Learning

For new learning to take place, your brain must remain alert and receptive. Stimulating the Reticular Activating System alerts the cognitive parts of your brain to get prepared for incoming data. When you move, you interrupt old patterns of behavior and clear the way for new ones. In Chapter 2, I noted that areas in the brain related to muscle movement are also essential in coordinating thought. In other words, vestibular stimulation movements such as infant crawling, learning to walk, and playing games deliver *pattern interrupts* that suspend ordinary sensory motor activities, permitting fresh patterns to emerge.

Childhood ear infections can impact vestibular processing, causing problems in later life such as difficulty with language, hyperactivity, focus difficulties, decrease in learning receptivity, and personality conflicts. These symptoms can become severe stressors in daily life, and interfere with the learning process.

Rayma Ditson-Sommer PhD of the Opnet Mental Training Institute in Phoenix AZ, uses vestibular stimulation by means of the "Symmetron" chair and motion bed in training professional and Olympic athletes. These movement devices help circulate fluids through the body and brain. This provides additional oxygen and nutrients to help alter perceptions, thus allowing athletes to respond differently to stimuli in the environment. The circular motion, coupled with specific light and sound, stimulates the brain and alters chemistry. While all of this is happening, the athlete visualizes perfect performances. (See the information in Chapter 9 on *light and sound* relating to hypnosis and trance.)

Any training or rehabilitation program can be enhanced through the use of vestibular-neuro-technological approaches. Posture and balance influence muscle activities throughout our lifetimes, and there is an elaborate interplay between mind, body, sensations, and movement. It is movement that integrates information of our experiences from our minds and bodies into our neural networks.

Studies at the Salk Institute in La Jolla, California, investigated the role of exercise, in particular running, on cell growth in lab animals. They showed that running increases the genesis and survival of new cells in the hippocampus, a region important for learning and memory. Active mice performed better on spatial learning tasks when compared to sedentary control mice. This study supports the notion that motion can enhance cognition.

In addition, Dr. Debbie Crews of Arizona State University, and her colleagues, ran a study in which a class of high school students was divided into two groups. The first group participated in an aerobic exercise program where instructors kept the students' heart rate above 140 beats per minute. The other group participated in a physical activity where their heart rate was kept below 140 beats per minute. Each group met three days a week for six weeks. The aerobic group had a statistically greater improvement in grades compared to those who participated in the simpler physical activity. The aerobic group also experienced lower depression and increased self-esteem. Although the science behind this is still unclear, one leading theory is that exercise provides the brain with more *glucose*. The brain needs glucose both to power neurons and to produce *acetylcholine*, a neurotransmitter important to memory. Naturally, the additional oxygen being supplied to the brain is also a factor.

We Are All Wired Differently

So far, this chapter has covered how movement benefits learning. Now I will narrow the focus to examine why some people may respond to the same stimulus in different ways. Although there may be numerous factors to account for these differences, in this section we will be looking at the way a brain is physically configured, and how that can be altered.

For the past forty years, there has been great emphasis on the function of different areas of the brain in relation to learning. As discussed in Chapter 2, the majority of people have a dominant left hemisphere of the neo-cortex. They tend to process information analytically and sequentially. Those who are right-hemisphere dominant tend to see the whole, and are more comfortable with music, art, and spatial relationships. In steady state, most people tend to process information using both sides of their brain.

In her book, *The Dominance Factor*, neurophysiologist Carla Hannaford explains how individuals have not only a dominant brain hemisphere and hand but also possess a dominant foot, eye, and ear.

Dominance is suspected to begin in utero. As early as nine weeks after conception, the *Moro Reflex* (a startle reflex) is established in the embryo. A newborn will employ its dominant ear to detect danger by resting its head with the dominant ear facing upward. This survival system incorporates the hands, feet, eyes, nose, and the proprioceptors (position sensors). During stress, people mechanically revert to their dominant sides. This is known as *basal dominance patterns*. Observing how their body and mind process information, a unique learning style is revealed. The various neural wiring configurations of the human brain, eye, ear, hand, and foot result in a total of thirty-two possible basal dominance profiles.

Basal Dominance Profiles as Learning Styles

Like any system that classifies preferences, styles or types, these profiles are not meant to be used as simple labels, which tend to confine and limit. Rather, the profiles provide self-knowledge and constructive insight so that both learners and instructors can understand where the academic and personal strengths and limitations are. In this way, incongruity between teaching methods and learning styles can be addressed. Lateral dominance profiles have far-reaching effects on our interpersonal activities, our decision-making, our problem-solving, our recreation, our perceptions, and, of course, our learning. Especially significant is that the way we are wired also affects how we manage stressors. The fundamental point in studying dominance is that while **learning new information, or under stress, people tend to depend on their dominant sides**. The non-dominant part is sidelined and may ultimately atrophy if this situation becomes enduring.

Each hemisphere of the brain controls most of the senses and motor functions on the opposite side of the physical body. This *cross-lateral* control means that if a dominant hand, foot, eye, or ear is on the opposite side to the dominant brain hemisphere, then neural transmission is maximized, even in times of stress.

If a dominant eye, ear, foot, or hand is found on the same side as the dominant hemisphere, then information processing is compromised, especially when learning new things or during stress. This is known as being *homo-laterally* wired. This may be one explanation for the internal representational preferences of NLP: visual, auditory, and kinesthetic. (See NLP in Chapter 10.) An example of this is when a person's eye, ear, and brain hemisphere are all dominant on the right side. During stress, this person would be unable to access most auditory and visual information, thus finding it difficult to communicate. This type of learner is unable to perceive the details and becomes overwhelmed, requiring quiet time alone to process the stimulation. Characteristically, this type of learner is branded "learning disabled," thereby intensifying the anxiety. Another example may be a person who is dominant left-brain, left hand, and left foot. This person, although being able to communicate just fine, would be unable to move in a coordinated manner.

Although the method in biokinesiology of muscle-testing may be used to determine dominance, simpler methods are explained in the following sections. Generally, children are easier to assess since they haven't a lifetime of developing stable compensating strategies.

To get a handle on which side of your brain tends to dominate, experiment with many of the free online tests available. Do a search on "brain dominance test." I recommend that you take them a number of times, and always in context (parent, student, work, social, volunteer, etc.). Keep a record of your scores in specific contexts. Do the tests over and over again, days and weeks apart. Eventually, you will understand clearly your brain dominance. Keep in mind that you may be fairly evenly balanced.

Take a look again at Table 2.1 – *Traits Of Opposing Brain Hemispheres* on page 36. Now think about how you react to stressful situations.

Visual

Only 4 percent of vision actually comes through the eyes. The other 96 percent is manufactured and processed within the mind using information from memories and the other senses. Almost half of all people are visually homo-lateral (dominant eye on the same side as their dominant brain hemisphere). This means that under stress or when learning new material, visual information is not readily available for processing.

Reading can be further complicated, since the dominant eye leads the tracking (coordination of both eyes). The right eye normally tracks from left to right. That's fine for those reading languages written in that direction. However, those with a left dominant eye, which tracks from right to left, will have trouble with English, but not Arabic or any other language written from right to left. Furthermore, since the hand and eye are so intimately linked, letter reversals are common when left eye dominant learners begin to read and write.

To reveal which eye is dominant, hold your thumb at arm's length and, while focusing on the thumb with both eyes open, line it up with some vertical object. Keeping the arm and head position fixed, alternately close each eye while keeping the other open. The eye that still sees the thumb lined up with the vertical object is the dominant eye.

The following table will give you some indication of how your eye dominance could influence your learning.

	DOMINANT LEFT BRAIN	DOMINANT RIGHT BRAIN
DOMINANT LEFT EYE	• Visual access limited during stress • May have to shut eyes to learn verbal information • Difficulty with reading/writing English	• Learns well visually even under stress • Difficulty with reading/writing English • Letter reversals common
DOMINANT RIGHT EYE	• Learns well visually even under stress • Difficulty reading languages written right to left	• Visual access limited during stress • May have to shut eyes to learn verbal information

Table 8.1   Faculties for Visual Channel Under Stress

Auditory

The temporal lobe deciphers sound information. Like all senses, it has strong neural links to the limbic system, which processes emotions and memory. Over half of learners are homo-lateral, which causes some memory challenges. Those whose dominant ear is cross-lateral to their dominant hemisphere, have a good facility for memory. Just what type of memory ability they have depends on which hemisphere is dominant. The following chart delineates what type of memory that is functional for each cross-lateral type.

In order to discover which ear is dominant, pretend that a soft conversation is taking place on the other side of a wall. Move forward with the intention of placing an ear on the wall. Whichever ear is presented to the wall is the dominant ear. Which ear you use when listening on the phone may also be an indication of your dominant ear.

	DOMINANT LEFT BRAIN	DOMINANT RIGHT BRAIN
DOMINANT LEFT EAR	• Memory challenges during stress and when learning new material	• Good memory for faces, meanings, emotions and whole concepts
DOMINANT RIGHT EAR	• Good memory for numbers formulas spelling and details	• Memory challenges during stress and when learning new material

Table 8.2 Memory Faculties for Auditory Channel Under Stress

Hands

When a person speaks, there is increased activity in the area of the brain associated with hand movements – the motor and sensory zones of the neo-cortex. Kinesthetic expression includes writing and body language like facial expressions and gestures. The following table displays how stress impacts communication skills as related to brain and hand dominance patterns.

Generally, the hand with which a person writes is the dominant hand. To check other people, you can present a small object, such as a pen, to them about waist level in the middle part of their torso. Whichever hand they use to grab the object is their dominant hand.

	DOMINANT LEFT BRAIN	DOMINANT RIGHT BRAIN
DOMINANT LEFT HAND	• Communication Limited	• Kinesthetically able • Verbally limited
DOMINANT RIGHT HAND	• Verbally able • Kinesthetically limited	• Communication limited

Table 8.3 Faculties for Hand Dominance Under Stress

Feet

Determining the dominant foot is as easy as stepping up on a chair. The foot used is the dominant foot. Another method is, with feet together, lean forward and see which foot jumps out to avoid a fall.

	DOMINANT LEFT BRAIN	DOMINANT RIGHT BRAIN
DOMINANT LEFT FOOT	• Difficulty taking action • Paralyzed, clumsy, awkward	• Spontaneous • Enjoy free-form • Don't easily follow instructions
DOMINANT RIGHT FOOT	• Plan their movements • Good at following instructions	• Difficulty taking action • Paralyzed, clumsy, awkward

Table 8.4   Faculties for Foot Dominance Under Stress

Your own Dominance Factor determines how well you handle learning new material and stress. If you would like to explore this subject in more depth, I recommend Dr. Hannaford's book, *The Dominance Factor.*

Creating Whole-Brain Integration

The optimal learning state is through integrated whole mind-body processing. With both hemispheres actively firing, access to all sensory information is certain. The synergy created through communication, processing, and action is maximized.

When you perform the following activities, you will be more centered, more coordinated, and less stressed. Your learning ability will be enhanced through the integration of the left and right hemispheres of your brain. Dee Coulter, a cognitive specialist and neuroscience educator, calls these exercises *micro-interventions*. Their success can also reverse a learner's expectation of failure.[35]

The origins of the following processes go back many thousands of years. Many organizations use movement to help people with diagnosed learning difficulties. Some of the various methods are know as Tactile Neurokinesiology Therapy, Proprioception Therapy, and Kinesiological and Neurokinesiological Rehabilitation.

According to specialized kinesiology researchers, 80 percent of learning difficulties are related to blockages generated by stress that short-circuits the brain. These fused electrical patterns can be released through competent use of kinesiology, including using pressure-points, muscle testing, and coordinated patterned movements.[36] In Chapter 5, we covered the Emotional Freedom Technique that also clears these neural short-circuits. Also, investigate local practitioners of Pilates, Craniosacral Therapy, Yoga, Tai Chi, and Brain Gym®.[37]

Tips to Aid in Clearer Thinking

Before beginning any energy work, the body must be properly hydrated. Sipping water regularly keeps the mind–body alert and energized. Remember what we discussed about the effects of dehydration on thinking.

Three slow deep breaths will rapidly bring your body into a relaxed state. You may have noticed babies lying on their back in a crib. Their bellies rise as they breathe. They are not breathing into their stomach. They are simply using their diaphragms to push their stomach out of the way to make room for their lungs to take in more air.

Cross-Crawl

Although this is generally done in a standing position, you can sit on a chair or stool if you like. Cross-crawl excites the vestibular system, the frontal lobes, the cerebellum, and the basal ganglia. This exercise facilitates balanced nerve activation across the corpus callosum. Done on a regular basis, you will experience faster and more integrated communication, improved focus and concentration, boosted metabolism and overall energy. You will have better coordination and balance, enhanced breathing, greater stamina, and even a greater ability to heal.

To do the cross-crawl, touch your right knee with your left hand or elbow, and then your left knee with your right hand or elbow. Ensure that your arm crosses the body's midline. It's like marching in place.

A baby crawling on all-fours, a cross-lateral movement, stimulates development of the *corpus callosum*, which contains the nerve pathways between the two hemispheres. This action gets both sides of the body working together, integrating the brain with the arms, legs, eyes, and ears.

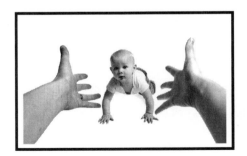

Eye Exercises

You may have noticed that when people talk, their eyes move from side to side. This is an indication that they are accessing different parts of their brain. If we deliberately move our eyes while thinking about something, we are purposefully calling on different parts of the brain to supply us with elusive memories, and to give us new insight. This is evidenced by the number of therapies that use eye movements to clear neural restrictions and blockages. Among them are EMDR (Eye Movement Desensitization and Reprocessing), Rapid Eye Therapy, and some of the energy psychologies.

To perform these exercises, keep your head straight and in line with your spine. Begin by looking straight ahead. Inhale, and then gently exhale as you move your eyes to one of the outer points listed below. Hold your breath for a few seconds and then return your eyes to the center while you inhale. Continue with another point. The points are up, down, right, left, up–right 45 degrees, down–left 45 degrees, down–right 45 degrees, and up–left 45 degrees. You can also do large circles in each direction, triangles, and lazy eights.

Rubs, Taps, and Pressure

In studying acupuncture, we learn about specific points along the energy meridians. Some of these points can also be activated by rubs, taps (EFT – Emotional Freedom Technique), simple pressure (acupressure), or even the new LifeWave[39] non-transdermal energy patches. Most likely, you will experience an immediate surge of energy. There are also cumulative effects, so over time, you will find yourself more focused, energized, and optimistic.

One of the most remarkable methods that I've learned is called *30 More Miles*. Not only will it relieve fatigued or restless legs, but it will also energize your whole body. In a sitting position, find the little bump just below, and on the outside of one knee. Now, form your hands into fists and thump both sides of your leg just below the knee, about the level of where that bump is. Keep this going for about 30 seconds or more. Now do the next leg. I love this for hiking and restless leg syndrome.

There are powerful points just under the clavicle, or collarbone. The acupuncturists call them K–27. To locate them, place the tips of your index fingers on the U–shaped notch at the top of the breastbone. Then move your fingers down over the collarbone, out to each side about an inch, into the soft tissue under the clavicle to the left and right of the sternum. Most people have small depressions there.

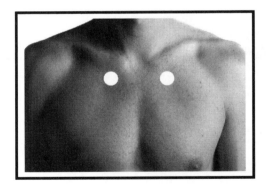

You can thump or rub these points. Either of these actions will increase the blood flow to the brain, resulting in more available oxygen. Do this exercise before reading to reduce eye strain. If you do the eye patterns, especially the "lazy eight" (∞) as you thump or rub, you will improve coordination between the left and right hemispheres of your brain. This may be as easy (or difficult) as rubbing your tummy and patting your head at the same time! Avoid this one just before to going to sleep.

Another interesting thump is known as the Tarzan Thump or Thymus Thump. The author of *Life Energy*, Dr. John Diamond, said that the thymus gland monitors and regulates the body's energy flow. Locate your thymus point just beneath the upper part of the breastbone in the middle of the chest. Thump in the middle of your chest with either your fingertips or your fist while taking three deep breaths. This is another one to avoid before bedtime.

Hook-Ups

Hook-ups can quickly counteract stress, sadness, confusion, and anger, all of which affect learning. They activate the sensory and motor cortices of each brain hemisphere. Among the various hook-ups available, I recommend the one known as "Cook's Hook Up". Here are the simple steps —

1. Place your tongue on the roof of your mouth just behind the teeth. This joins the emotional limbic system and the logical frontal lobes.

2. Cross your ankles, and extend your hands, palms facing outward. Cross your wrists with the thumbs pointing down and clasp your hands. Then bend your elbows and fold your joined hands against your chest.

3. Deep breathe for one or two minutes. A feeling of a focused calm will come over you.

This complex crossover action has a similar integrative effect in the brain as the cross-crawl. You can experiment with crossing left over right or right over left to see which is better for you.

B locked sinus cavities and eustachian tubes can literally muddle thinking. A simple procedure for clearing the head is to snort about a teaspoon of <u>very slightly</u> salted warm water into each nostril. The solution will easily flush the nasal passages, almost certainly resulting in improved breathing, eyesight, and hearing.[38] If you have any concern about this, ask your physician.

Conclusion

How the brain operates is currently one of the most active fields of scientific research. As new imaging technology reveals more about the dynamic links between mind and body, we can then approach the whole subject of learning and memory in fresh ways. For example, movement stimulates the growth of nerve cells, thus, influencing learning. Through understanding your own unique neural configuration, you can alter your methods of studying to maximize your strengths.

I recommend daily use of the brain integration exercises, particularly prior to work or study.

1. **What is your greatest learning from this chapter?**

2. **What is one thing that you would like to change about your life that would bring you greater success and peace of mind?**

3. **CALL TO ACTION:**
   Visit <u>www.UnleashingBook.com</u> to link to the CLI site. Choose the free self-coaching tool entitled "The Brain Walk® – A Journey for Peace of Mind." This tool will provide you with much clarity on your life's direction, and solutions to achieve your personal goals.

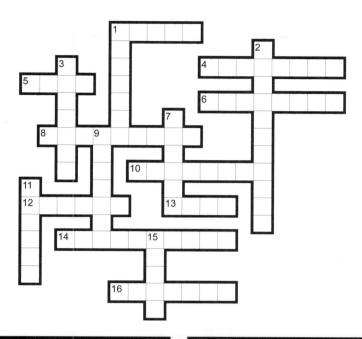

ACROSS

1. Eyes movement: accesses different parts of the _____
4. Learning new info, or stressed, people depend on their _____ side
5. 30 More Miles requires thumping around the _____
6. Kinesiology: is simply the study of body _____
8. In homeostasis: processing is in _____ _____ of the brain
10. Drives infants' learning
12. 'Tarzan Thump' gland
13. Dominant right-brain/ dominant _____ foot, don't easily follow instructions
14. _____ system controls sense of movement and balance
16. Brain areas for movement, also synchronize _____

DOWN

1. Three slow deep _____ will relax the body very quickly
2. The study of body language, physical exercise, anatomy, and physiology.
3. Nerve cells adapted for transmission of electrical messages throughout the body
7. Movement integrates mind & body info into our _____ networks
9. _____ activate the sensory and motor cortices of each brain hemisphere.
11. 80% of learning blockages are generated by _____
15. Thumping K-27 sends more _____ to the brain

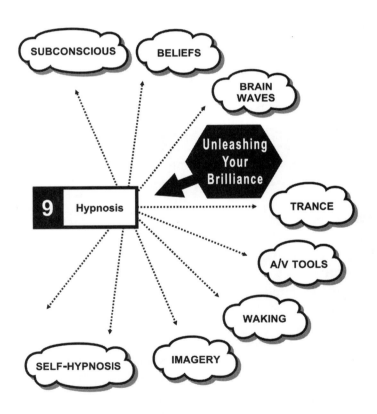

HYPNOSIS

> *We are what we repeatedly do.*
> *Excellence then is not an act,*
> *but a habit.*
>
> Aristotle

Contrary to the myths found in books, on the stage, and in movies, hypnosis is a natural state that all of us experience every day. Some forms of the hypnotic state that you experience are driving a car and then realizing that you were not consciously aware of the past few miles, the dreamy state as you awaken in the morning or the middle of the night, and simple daydreaming. Hypnosis is an altered state that is typified by increased suggestibility due to the bypass of the critical faculty, as mentioned in Chapter 4.

Although formal hypnotic induction requires specialized training, teachers and learners can easily employ some of the methods outlined within this chapter. Initially, I will describe how the subconscious and conscious minds interact. I will then explain how beliefs are formed, how brain waves can indicate the degree of subconscious activity, and what *trance* **is. The techniques will then be reviewed, including audio-visual tools, waking hypnosis, imagery, and self-hypnosis.**

One of the most powerful conscious skills available to humankind is the ability to selectively focus for extended periods of time without interruption – This just happens to be one of the most difficult skills for people to master. Wandering minds and external stimulations constantly distract, contaminating the input of study or work. Hypnosis and self-hypnosis can improve conscious concentration through post-hypnotic suggestion. As well, anyone can be taught how to relax the mind to enhance creativity and more successfully absorb information without the persistent jamming by the critical faculty.

A study during the 2000–2001 academic year was undertaken with six psychology classes at South Piedmont Community College in Polkton, North Carolina. The purpose was to determine how effective hypnosis was in improving academic results. It focused on general learning, study habits, memory, and test-taking. The extracurricular hypnosis sessions used direct suggestion. The results revealed that the experimental group received a full letter grade higher than the group who were not hypnotized.[40]

Effective learning incorporates a cluster of factors. Before considering specific techniques to enhance scholastic ability, it is useful for the student to develop a solid foundation of intention, motivation, well-considered goals, secure self-esteem, discipline, and organization. Hypnosis is excellent in clarifying and enhancing all of these. Difficulties with moods, sleep deprivation, self-sabotage, and negative emotions are usually handled concurrently when hypnosis and self-hypnosis are undertaken. Hypnosis can also help learning by improving study and reading skills, enhancing memory, and reducing test anxiety. Hypnosis also encourages the integration of new material by facilitating associations with already-learned information.

The Relationship Between the Subconscious and Conscious Mind

In hypnosis, there are two principles of the subconscious mind.

- The *agreement principle* says that the subconscious mind always follows what it is instructed to do.

- The *compliance principle* says that the subconscious mind always moves in the direction in which the conscious mind points it.

These principles depend on the conviction that whatever is strongly believed becomes reality. The way a people **think** they can learn will largely determine the way they **will** learn. The subconscious mind has properties much different from those of the conscious mind. Examine the parallels between this table and those of opposing brain hemispheres in Chapter 2.

CONSCIOUS	SUBCONSCIOUS
Active and controlling	Receptive, spontaneous, participatory
Deeper into detail (Analytical)	Considers the big picture (Gestalt)
Competitive	Collaborative
External	Internal
From parts to whole	From whole to parts
Misinterprets instructions	Responds literally
Objective	Subjective
Obsessed with correctness	Takes path of least resistance
Rational and Logical	Irrational
Serial and linear	Parallel and seeks links
Specific	Ambiguous
Temporary memory	Permanent memory
Thoughtful	Emotional
Willpower	Habits and patterns

Table 9.1   Traits of the Conscious and Subconscious Minds

Beliefs

What good is a belief if it does not benefit your life?

Phineas Parkhurst Quimby, 1862

Self-imposed boundaries or limitations are often present because of established beliefs. Once beliefs are accepted as fact, only a paradigm shift will shape a change. Remember the story of the elephant in the introduction?

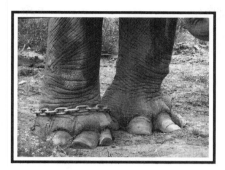

To help people shift out of a stuck attitude, therapists use a technique known as *"Gradually enlarging the possibility."* Subjects are asked to recognize the dissimilarity between their alleged limit and a point that is a preposterously small fraction beyond that. Of course, the subjects shrug off this minimal difference as insignificant; therefore, the new frontier is achieved. This process continues in nominal increments until the difference is significant and the subjects have mentally accepted the new possibility – the new "limit".

Whether or not they are aware of them, teachers possess a full set of beliefs that are conflicting and congruent to different extents. In the 1968 study, *The Pygmalion Effect,* Rosenthal and Jacobson found that the power of teacher beliefs shaped student results. Harvard researchers gave a group of students an achievement test, and told teachers it was a test to predict future progress. They picked names **at random** and told the teachers that specific students would make amazing progress that year. At the end of the year, the researchers returned with a follow-up test. They found that the selected students had made more progress than the students who were not chosen. The "difference that made the difference" was the set of teachers' expectations, which were unconsciously communicated to the students. In actuality, this is a special form of hypnosis, *waking hypnosis,* which is described later in this chapter.

Brain Waves

Every level of awareness, including thought, feeling, and
sensation has a corresponding brain wave pattern.

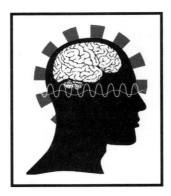

- Infants are born into, and operate at, a very slow frequency called *Delta*. Adults can reach this state during deep
sleep, or when they're feeling a detached awareness.

- Around the age of four, a young child's brain frequency
increases, allowing it to also function in the *Theta* state.
Adults, during light or medium sleep, or when in a meditative or hypnotic state, experience the Theta state. It
is the same tempo as that of the constant and rhythmic
drone chanted by Tibetan monks.

- At about the age of seven, the child's brain has the ability
to perform at an even faster frequency, known as *Alpha*.
This highly suggestible, daydreaming state is excellent
for imagery, learning facts, synthesizing new knowledge, strengthening long-term memory, and nurturing
creativity.

- At about the age of fourteen, the child's brain reaches the
ability to function in the *Beta* state. This is the alert, conscious or "wide-awake" state that we tend to experience
for much of the time we are awake.

In Chapter 2, we discussed the Basic Rest–Activity Cycle. During the daytime, the **active** (left–brain) cycle is typified by beta brain waves and the **rest** (right–brain) cycle exhibits Alpha brain waves. It is during this rest phase that daydreaming takes place. While asleep or in deep trance, the oscillation operates between theta and delta waves. (See Chapter 2 *Whole-Brain Learning – Hemispheric Dominance*)

Those categories of brain waves that are slower than beta waves indicate levels of trance and can be reached through formal hypnotic induction, meditation, or simple relaxation. The following chart displays the number of times a suggestion must be repeated to shape a change in behavior. Notice that affirmations expressed in the fully conscious (Beta) state require thousands of repetitions to be effective.

BRAIN WAVE	CYCLES PER SECOND	USUAL STATE FOR ADULTS	AGE THIS FIRST APPEARS	REPS REQUIRED FOR NEW BEHAVIOR
Beta 2	> 21	• High stress • Extremely narrow focus	—	—
Beta	14 – 21	• Normal waking alertness	14 +	Thousands
Alpha	7 – 13	• Daydream • Creative • Highly suggestible	4 – 7	About 21
Theta	4 – 7	• Light sleep	4 – 7	1 – 2
Delta	0.5 – 4	• Dreamless deep sleep • Cell-regeneration	0 – 4	—

Table 9.2   Brain Wave Frequencies and Associated Activities

What is Trance?

Trance is a natural state that is often achieved while simply performing natural activities. Examples include sitting at the keyboard for long periods, long-distance running, watching television, and daydreaming. Many of these happen during the rest phase of the Basic Rest Activity Cycle, as discussed in Chapter 2.

People often ask me what the difference is between a meditation trance and a hypnosis trance. The trance itself is the same, and methods to reach trance vary within each activity. Some meditative practices are intended to allow participants to attain a place of peace or bliss. Other types of meditation function like hypnosis, to release limiting beliefs, negative habits or behaviors, and to replace them with positive useful ones.

Professor Thomas H. Budzynski, of the University of Washington refers to *hypnagogic*, *reverie*, and *transliminal* states as the twilight states of consciousness. He says they aid in the absorption and retrieval of material since they are relaxed rather than competitive, and that these states are valuable, since learning appears to be a holistic or intuitive phenomenon.[41]

If you are one of those people who wake up in the middle of the night and can't get back to sleep, chances are that this is one of the most creative periods in your day. *Carpe Diem* (*Seize the Day!*) Exploit this opportunity to tap into your subconscious thoughts. I do some of my most inspired work in the middle of the night. I keep a pad and pen next to my bed, as well as a digital audio recorder. Another excellent use of this trance state is to express your goals. You can even play back some pre-recorded affirmations.

I shut my eyes in order to see.

Paul Gauguin

Benefits of Trance

When in a sufficiently deep trance, you can realize a number of benefits:

- Your subconscious is one-hundred to two hundred times more susceptible to suggestions.

- The critical faculty (explained in Chapter 4), which normally blocks access to your subconscious mind, is bypassed, and you can more easily draw upon greater knowledge in an area of focus.

- There is a striking increase in the manufacture of valuable brain chemicals, including those that slow aging, increase longevity, and provide a feeling of well-being.

- With the right conditions, there may be a release of dysfunctional and limiting mental and emotional patterns, such as anger, fear, anxiety, depression, guilt, sadness, and self-sabotage.

- You experience greater whole-brain functioning, resulting in improved focus and concentration, greater intuition, increased learning ability, enhanced creativity, and improved self-awareness.

- You experience markedly lower stress levels, greater clarity, and calmness. You feel more relaxed, less anxious, more centered, more peaceful, and more connected to others.

- Risk-taking seems less intimidating.

- While your aliveness, vitality and energy increase, your need for sleep decreases.

My clients often tell me how pleased they are to have been introduced to hypnosis. I conduct many different kinds of workshops, yet the one that I enjoy teaching the most is self-hypnosis. Apart from some goal-setting instruction and other necessary explanations, most of the class time is in trance.

Trance can be induced through progressive relaxation, boredom, shock, misdirection, and confusion. (See *Milton Model* in Chapter 10) Although hypnotic sound recordings have been around for decades, new technology has recently taken this to a new level. I will review some of these here.

Audio & Visual Trance Tools

If you haven't had the opportunity to learn self-hypnosis, the tools described below will get you into trance efficiently. For your convenience, I have placed links to their sites on this book's web site – www.UnleashingBook.com In addition to what you find here; there are thousands of products available that feature a hypnotist gently guiding you through a progressive relaxation. Many of them include visualizations and suggestions for such things as better health and more confidence.

Audio Tools

Enhancer – One of the foremost architects of this medium is author and seminar leader Dick Sutphen. With nineteen books and over thirty CD titles to his credit, Sutphen is considered a leader in this field. For academic endeavors, *Enhancer* particularly stands out. Crafted as an "eyes-open" trance inducer, it is able to take a listener to mid-level theta, while at the same time maintaining an alert and focused attention. You can easily enter the flow state, where productivity rises and time seems to disappear. My own experience with this product has allowed me to write and plan more efficiently. With the Enhancer in the background, I have been able to concentrate on a paper, and the first thing I would notice was the recycling of the CD after seventy-four minutes. I would then realize how much work I had produced without distraction.

Inner Peace Music – Developed by Steve Halpern, another innovator in this field. His company offers tapes and CDs to enhance accelerated learning, creativity, and self-esteem. As he states in his web site, "This music assisted over 85 percent of test subjects to effortlessly enter Alpha and Theta brainwave states, and experience hemispheric synchronization."

The Holosync Solution® – This system has been developed by Centerpointe Research Institute of Beaverton, Oregon. It is not a hypnosis product per se. The listeners' nervous systems receive a very specific audio stimulus through each ear that takes them into a state of deep meditation. In order to process and handle this stimulus, an individual's brain will create new neural pathways between the left and right sides of the brain. (See Chapter 2 on *Whole-Brain Learning – Hemispheric Dominance*) Over time, it creates a new structure that can easily handle the stimulus in the program, requiring a subscriber to progress to the next level. As the brain waves slow from beta to alpha to theta to delta, there is a corresponding increase in balance between the two hemispheres of the brain. What is taking place is that the program is gradually giving the nervous system more input (of a very precise nature) than it can handle. Its current neurological structure is altered, pushing it to grow stronger. The increased communication between the left and right hemispheres of the brain leads to whole-brain functioning. Whole-brain functioning is associated with increased creativity, insight, learning ability, problem solving ability, and memory. (See chapter 8)

Learning Strategies Corporation has now added the Holosync® audio technology to their Paraliminal audio series.

Audio-Visual Tools

Light and sound – Mental tuning helps to develop a calm, quiet mind. This is where focus, concentration, visualization, and positive attitudes all reside. The technology incorporates two slightly different tones, one in each ear. These barely-perceptible alternating tones are tuned to specific frequencies, and work in concert with the LED lights, which are placed in specially-designed glasses. One set of glasses is blacked-out, and is intended for visualization and affirmation. The other style of glasses, specifically designed for reading, has the tiny lights placed around clear openings to permit reading in an altered state, which will enhance the efficacy of a study session.

By means of process or end-result visualization, you can imagine your successful progress or completion of a project, course, or degree. This process will also have an effect in overcoming self-sabotage. Visualizing excellent performance in presentations or exams can also set anchors, such as confidence, enhanced alertness, or relaxation.

AV3x – The Innerscape Adventure – This DVD combines animated, morphing imagery and ethereal soundscapes of nature and music with alpha/theta brainwave stimulation to create a powerful relaxation. It has been developed by Christopher Oliver, a pioneer in the field of mind machines and audio/visual brainwave stimulation. Its six tracks are Exploration, Enchantment, Transcendence, Rebirth, Serenity, and Regeneration.

Psychovisual Therapy – This DVD product is designed to deal with specific issues such as Self-Confidence, Weight Control, and Stress Control. Embedded in the video are simple subliminal video messages. Success requires watching it many times. Two titles that you may find helpful are *Serenity* and *Relax and Let Go*.

If you are unable to visit a hypnotherapist or attend a self-hypnosis class, these audio-visual products will help you reach the goals you set for yourself.

Waking Hypnosis

> *A powerful agent is the right word.*
> Samuel Langhorne Clemens

> *Kind words can be short and easy to speak,*
> *but their echoes are truly endless.*
> Mother Theresa

When suggestions bypass the critical faculty without the benefit of trance, this is called waking hypnosis. Under the right conditions of rapport, a person can exercise extreme influence over others by implanting selective thinking. In order to bypass the critical faculty, the subject must not be resistant to the suggestion on the conscious level. Generally, the person making the suggestions is held in kind regard or esteem. Many parents, teachers, coaches, older siblings, and others fail to appreciate that, to the listener's subconscious, their simple words can have considerable sway. In his book *Hypnotherapy*, Dave Elman said, "To cause the human to lock around a given idea, suggestions in the waking state must be given with complete confidence; with absolute assurance. They must leave no room for doubt. If doubt creeps in, the suggestion usually becomes ineffective." Waking hypnosis is probably the simplest, the most effective, and most underutilized method of achieving positive hypnotic results without the necessity of trance.

Many of the skills that people possess are habits and attitudes that have been picked up during their youth. Supervisors and instructors, if aware of the Basic Rest Activity Cycle (discussed in Chapter 2), know that their employees or learners enter a suggestible state often. They can capitalize on that fact to influence attitudes, behaviors, and habits. Since they are in positions of authority and are allotted a great deal of time to communicate with their charges, they are extremely well-placed to provide messages that can stimulate more effective performance.

In the book *The One-Minute Manager*, Ken Blanchard recommends catching them doing something right – and acknowledge them. Very powerful.

Through the use of distinctive language, teachers can shift the students' focus from previously-experienced discomfort and self-doubt, to more confident and proactive images and outcomes. This new focus will encourage the students' ability to learn, and empower them to make their experience educationally enriching. For example, Robyn Mor, a teacher friend of mine, told me that she used to attempt bonding with her students through expressing empathy. She would say, "I know this is difficult. Do your best." Now she uses more encouraging language such as, "We've covered all this material, and I know that you'll just fly through it and turn in great papers." By expanding the students' ability to hold these newer more useful patterns in consciousness for longer periods, Robyn's students will tend to automatically and effortlessly let go of the older, less-effective patterns.

Everything we do and say transmits information. All language, whether written, spoken, or conveyed through body language, creates internal representations in those who read, hear, or see what we have sent. These internal representations may or may not be accurate.

The principle idea behind educational hypnosis is the desire to consistently suggest internal representations that lead someone to either maintain positive behaviors or replace negative behaviors with constructive ones.

Imagery

Imagery is a part of the mental coding system that blueprints behaviors. The broad term *imagery* is used to accommodate people who believe they cannot visualize a scene in their mind's eye.

Occasionally, in my self-hypnosis workshops, people tell me that they cannot visualize. I ask them how many windows face the street in the house they presently live. As soon as they give me an answer, they realize that to get that answer, they had to visualize the house itself. Visualization skills can be developed through proper training.

> *A person is literally what he thinks, his character being the complete sum of all his thoughts.*
>
> James Allen, in
> *As a Man Thinketh*

> *Imagination is more important than knowledge, for while knowledge points to all there is, imagination points to all there will be.*
>
> Albert Einstein

*Visualizing your future is
key to achieving phenomenal
wealth and success.*

Mark Victor Hansen,
co–author of *Chicken Soup for the Soul*

The most effective way to imagine is by recruiting all your senses. That is visual, auditory, kinesthetic (body sensations, feelings, and emotions), smell, and taste. Whichever way you do it, make it as vivid and real as possible. What you are doing here is directing the power of your subconscious mind. If it is running a program that says you're a "C" student, then that is what you will always be. That is, unless you convince your subconscious otherwise. If you vividly imagine something that doesn't match the template in the subconscious, eventually the subconscious is forced to amend its program. Effective imagery comes from well-formed goals. (See the section on goal-setting in Chapter 3.)

There are two categories of imagery, and each has its function.

- *Process imagery* is when you imagine being in the activity, such as attending a lecture, studying, or writing an exam. If these activities cause stress or are usually a difficulty, then you can imagine doing them flawlessly.

- *End result imagery* is effective when you imagine getting your paper back from the teacher and seeing a good score, or even receiving your diploma. By means of visualizing the goal as already having been achieved, expectancy is built up. The subconscious has no sense of time, so your vivid image, persistently used, will force the subconscious to create the means to get you there.

Metaphors

Aside from circumventing the critical faculty, storytelling presents metaphors for situations in people's lives. For millennia, narratives have been used to pass along ancestral history, practices, and values. In modern times, parents tell their children bedtime stories to inferentially impart societal values. The children's subconscious minds fill in the blanks and join the dots.

Whether fairy tales or anecdotes, the subconscious mind wants to make sense of the tale by discovering the deeper connotation. What's important is to ensure that the moral is not revealed to the conscious mind. If it is, then the subconscious mind, taking its traditional path of least resistance, will not bother processing and integrating. When Aesop misguidedly revealed the morals of his stories, his listeners' imaginations were not engaged at a level where the most benefit could occur.

When working with a client, a hypnotherapist ensures that the lessons are congruent with the client's values. The skill involved in creating a suitable metaphor, is to develop a narrative whose theme is obliquely parallel to the issue at hand. The conscious mind will attach to the literal superficial story, and the subconscious mind will hit upon the deeper, concealed message.

Self-Hypnosis

The central benefit of self-hypnosis is that it meets individual needs. The suggestions are purely subjective and are most effective when part of a well thought out plan of action.

The whole point of self-hypnosis is to take your goals or affirmations down into the trance with you. Check out your local hypnotherapists to see who offers self-hypnosis workshops. Once you have a well-crafted set of goals, you can easily convert them to suggestions for your subconscious mind. That's where all the action is.

A trainer or teacher would be wise to avoid words like hypnosis, trance, and induction, in favor of imagery, visualization, or relaxation. For the more sophisticated techniques, you can request the assistance of a certified hypnotherapist. When children are involved, parental permission is usually required. (Check www.UnleashingBook.com for links to professional hypnosis organizations)

Summary

There are many ways to use hypnosis to improve your performance. You can optimize your ability to cope with the demands of learning, as well as the stresses of being tested and judged on a fairly regular basis. Setting your mind in the direction of success, and putting aside negative self-talk is always helpful in maximizing performance.

> *The significant problems we face*
> *cannot be solved*
> *at the same level of thinking*
> *we were at when we created them.*
>
> Albert Einstein

1. What is your greatest learning from this chapter?

2. What is one thing you could do to make your life more meaningful?

3. **CALL TO ACTION:**
   Visit www.UnleashingBook.com to link to the CLI site. Choose the free self-coaching tool entitled "Goal Achiever." This tool will invite you to think about your goal of making your life more meaningful. Next, it will assist you in removing roadblocks to the achievement of that goal and provide you with solutions.

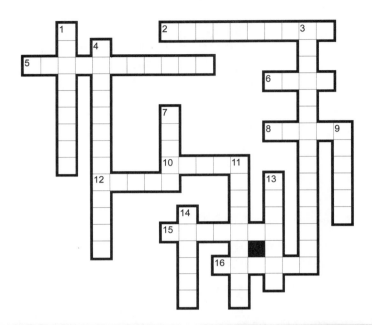

ACROSS

2. The subconscious mind always follows direction that the conscious mind points it
5. The subconscious mind wants to discover the deeper _____
6. The "wide-awake" state
8. In self-hypnosis take your _____ down into the trance with you
10. Same tempo as rhythmic drone of Tibetan monks
12. highly suggestible, day-dreaming state
15. imagery when you imagine being in the activity
16. Whole-brain functioning is results in increased _____

DOWN

1. Trance can be induced through _____
3. Normally block access to your subconscious mind
4. One of the greatest difficulties that students have
7. Infants operate at this very slow frequency
9. The most effective way to imagine is by recruiting all your _____
11. The subconscious mind always follows what it is instructed to do
13. Hypnosis is meditation with a _____
14. Slower than beta brain waves indicate _____

BRILLIANT NOTES

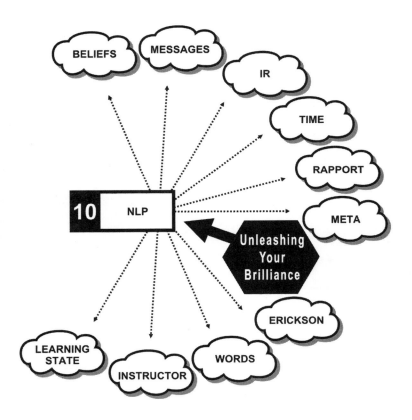

10

NLP - NEUROLINGUISTIC PROGRAMMING

> *We must learn to understand the "out–of–awareness" aspects of communication*
>
> Edward T. Hall

NLP, the study of subjective experience, provides a set of elegant communication and behavioral change tools. Co-developed in the early 1970s by a mathematician and a linguist, NLP is a model for understanding and duplicating excellence in human behavior. The material contained in this chapter benefit both trainer and learner.

We use our senses to explore and map the outside world. Our learning is shaped through unique experiences, culture, language, beliefs, values, interests, and assumptions. How we put these together determines how effective we are in achieving the results we want. We act on the basis of what we perceive. Sometimes our perceptions enrich us and sometimes they limit us. What do you perceive in the picture following?

In the 1970s, mathematician Richard Bandler and linguist John Grinder set out to study excellent communicators to find "the difference that makes the difference" between people who are exceptional, and those who are not. They proposed that people could become excellent by precisely modeling excellent people. The foremost models they studied were family therapist Virginia Satir, physician and hypnotherapist Milton Erickson, and Gestalt therapist Fritz Pearls. Contributing from an anthropological perspective were Edward T. Hall, Margaret Mead, and Gregory Bateson. This study evolved to what is now known as Neurolinguistic Programming.

NLP can improve learning and communication skills, as well as help conquer limitations such as conflicts, fears, and anxieties. Everyone's learning style is grounded in their belief of how they fit into society at large. In NLP, this is known as *model of the world*. This model is blended with a combination of perception, organization, and process of information. Being familiar with your own style can facilitate more effective learning.

Backbone Beliefs of NLP

We all have beliefs and expectations, so, if we have a preference, rather than focusing on those that limit us, we may as well embrace those that give us the most freedom.

The *Law of Requisite Variety* states that within a group of systems, the system with the most variability controls the system. In interpersonal terms, the person with the greatest flexibility controls the state of affairs.

Here are some NLP beliefs related to learning:

- Communication is two-way, and the response validates the message. Is what you think the instructor said really what was said or just your interpretation?

- Anything can be learned if it is broken down into smaller units. On both the practical and psychological levels, bite-sized tasks are more manageable.

- There are no mistakes, only outcomes. There are no failures, only lessons. Unfortunately, the impoverished feedback from some trainers and teachers contributes to stress and long-term dampening of self-esteem.

> *Failure is like fertilizer. It might stink, but it stimulates growth.*
>
> Anonymous

> *I never once failed; it took me thousands of steps to succeed. I learned a lot from the light bulbs that didn't work.*
>
> Thomas Edison

- People perform to the best of their ability with the tools they possess; however, they may not be in the resourceful state required to maximize their abilities. The most resourceful state for learning is relaxed alertness.

- If something can be learned by anyone else in the world, it is possible for you to learn. Accepting this can reduce any limiting beliefs you may have.

- Interpersonal communication is maximized when you respect others peoples' models of the world.

- The way we experience the world is only a perceptual model formed over the years, and perception can be changed.

- Resistance is not defiance, but simply a sign that rapport is lacking. Automatic behaviors are habitual patterns and not consciously intended. It is imperative to separate behavior from intention. This belief is especially important for instructor-learner communications.

- More choice is better than limited choice. All procedures should be designed to increase choices.

Messages Sent & Messages Received

NLP is built around the model that the human brain is a biological computer. Like all computers, it needs software to operate. The software that runs the brain is the fusion of external sensory input and our internal linguistic faculties. How we fashion our communications will do more to affect our outcomes than any other single factor. By changing our thoughts, we change our reality. If we know how another person thinks, we can change what we do to accommodate the needs of that person. This way, we have greater capacity to reach our goals in dealing with that person. NLP can be equated to a user's operation manual for the brain.

Excellent communicators appreciate that the *surface structure* of what is said does not necessarily convey the explicit meaning of the *deep structure*. In other words, ambiguity is a large part of every communication. (See *Meta Model* later in this chapter) Effective communicators are able to maximize the use of non-verbal language. They also understand that information is subject to generalization, deletion, and distortion during mental processing.

During their research, Bandler and Grinder discovered links between body postures, breathing patterns, and eye movements and various ways of thinking. These links, known as *Internal Representations*, are commonly categorized as *Visual, Auditory*, and *Kinesthetic*. Often included in the kinesthetic category are *smell* and *taste*. (See *Internal Representations as Learning Styles* below.)

One study revealed that 55 percent of messages are received because of posture, gestures, and eye contact; 38 percent is attributed to the tone of the presenter's voice; and only 7 percent is a result of the verbal content.[42] Teachers use some sort of non-verbal communication every ten to twelve seconds.[43]

Internal Representations as Learning Styles

> *People who learn to control inner experience will be able to determine the quality of their lives, which is as close as any of us can come to being happy. Although in its present state the human mind cannot do what some people would wish it to do, the mind has enormous untapped potential that we desperately need to learn how to use.*
>
> Mihaly Csikszentmihaly:
> *Flow, The Psychology of Optimal Experience*

Although most people use more than one Internal Representation system at any one time, many accentuate their preferred learning style to cope with specific conditions. In a typical classroom, some 20 percent of the learners will have access to only one system. Unless the lesson presented is in their preferred learning style, they are at a distinct disadvantage. Each style has a set of unique attributes.

> *We do not see things as they are,*
> *we see them as we are.*
>
> *Talmud*

Visual Learners

- Speak and read quickly. They would rather read than be read to, and remember what they see, rather than hear.

- Usually need to see it to learn it, and have difficulty following lectures.

- Often have difficulties with verbal directions, commonly misinterpreting words. They may forget verbal instructions unless they're written down.

- Need an overall view and purpose, and are cautious until mentally clear about an issue or project.

- Stand back when conversing, so as to "take it all in."

- Memorize by visual association.

- Are good spellers, and can actually see the words in their minds.

- Are good long-range planners and organizers.

- Are observant of environmental detail (e.g. body language, posters, lighting).

- Have a strong sense of color, and may have artistic abilities.

- Are neat, orderly, and appearance-oriented, in both dress and presentation.

- Are not usually distracted by noise.

- Often know *what* to say, yet can't think of the right words.

Learning tips for visual learners include using graphics (films, illustrations, and diagrams), color-coding notes and possessions, asking for written directions, employing concept maps and flow charts for outlines and note taking. Spelling can be improved by visualizing words.

Auditory Learners

- Need to hear something to learn it.

- May have difficulty with written directions, since reading might be a challenge.

- Find writing a challenge, and are better at communicating verbally. They can repeat back and mimic tone pitch and timbre, and speak in rhythmic patterns.

- Often have difficulty reading body language and facial expressions.

- Learn by listening, and remember what was discussed rather than seen.

- Can spell better orally than in written form.

- Talk to themselves while working, and move their lips and pronounce the words as they read.

- Are easily distracted by noise.

- Have problems with projects that involve visualization.

- Are frequently eloquent speakers, are talkative, love discussions, and go into lengthy descriptions. They enjoy reading aloud and listening.

To enhance their learning, auditory learners can have someone read, or record and play back, directions, review material, or test questions. Learning can also be helped through participation in discussions and interviews with appropriate parties. (See section on *Brain Specialization for Social Perception* in Chapter 2; see Chapter 12 on *Suggestopedia*.)

Kinesthetic Learners

- Learn by manipulating and doing, and can often assemble parts without directions of any kind.

- Speak slowly and use action words. They want to act things out.

- Stand close when talking to someone, and touch people to get their attention.

- May have messy handwriting.

- Memorize by walking and seeing, and are physically oriented.

- Learn more effectively when physically active, and can't sit still for long periods of time. They like involved games. They may be well coordinated and have athletic abilities.

- Can't remember geography unless they've actually been there.

- Enjoy plot-oriented books, and reflect action with facial expressions and gestures as they read. To maximize their learning, kinesthetic learners should focus on experiential activities such as role-playing, and lab work. Chewing gum, and taking frequent breaks during study periods will ensure that their pent-up energy is dissipated. Spelling and remembering facts can be enhanced through tracing letters and words. Memorization is bolstered through walking, dancing, drama, and exercising. The use of computers adds the kinesthetic touch.

Since traditional school curricula favor visual and auditory delivery, the kinesthetic learners are the ones that most often lose out. Numerous studies of "kids at risk" have shown that the vast majority of dropouts were kinesthetic learners.[44] They were unable to focus while sitting still for long periods. This behavior either got them into trouble or labeled "hyperactive."

Measures to stimulate whole-brain functioning can significantly enhance use of all three internal representation systems. (See Chapters 4 and 8.)

Auditory Digital Learners

Another lesser-known system, *Auditory Digital*, is not directly associated with any sensory system. It is common in people who tend to internalize and analyze information. They use their visual, auditory, and kinesthetic capacities in a balanced fashion. What can be helpful for Auditory Digital learners is to provide downtime periods for introspection and integration.

Is It That Late Already?

Most people are required to interact with others to accomplish tasks. Occasionally, these transactions go off track due to differences about how important time is. In their book, *Time Line Therapy and the Basis of Personality*, Tad James and Wyatt Woodsmall describe two main ways that people account for time in their lives.

Through Time people have a good sense of the sequential, linear nature of time. They keep appointments and expect others to do likewise. *In Time* people live in the now, so deadlines and appointments are low priorities.

Managers and trainers are wise to be aware of what their own type is, and of its influence on their employees and learners and the standards being set. In establishing deadlines, a *Through Time* manager or trainer must walk the fine line of making some allowances for *In Time* learners and, while still appearing fair-minded to the others. *In Time* managers or trainers must ensure that flexible and casual requirements do not instill attitudes of indifference or irresponsibility.

"Likes" Attract

People like people who are like themselves. When two people develop a sense of sameness or a shared experience, it is known as *rapport*. When rapport is well established, a manager's or instructor's credibility is instantly conveyed to the employees or learners, creating a sense of connection or flow. When this flow isn't evident, it can be a sign that rapport must be re-established. Focusing only on the subject material is not dynamic enough to create the flow. Achieving rapport is the ability to enter others' models of the world, and letting them know that we truly value their model.[45] It is a pattern that is sometimes expressed as:

I = YOU

MY IDEAS = YOUR IDEAS

MY MOVEMENTS = YOUR MOVEMENTS

MY STATE OF MIND = YOUR STATE OF MIND

The degree of rapport determines the degree of identification with others. The handshake in the West and the bow in Japan are both formal methods of creating this pattern.

Rapport can be easily and quickly established through assuming the posture or subtle motions and behaviors of another. This is known as *mirroring* and *matching*. Milton Erickson is considered the master of rapport. One method he used was to synchronize his breathing with that of a client. Sometimes, in lieu of breathing in sync, he moved his finger in time with the client's breathing. This is known as *crossover mirroring*. Although not noticed consciously, the client's peripheral vision would convey the information directly to the subconscious, thereby establishing rapport. This matching of another's model of the world is also known as *pacing*.

You can create rapport when you match another's tonality, use similar body language, or even squat to meet someone sitting eye-to-eye. As well, you can identify someone's preferred representational system by listening carefully to the words used. (See the next section on *verbal pacing*.) These skills are valuable for all aspects of social, family, and working life. No matter what your interests, you are interacting with people most of the time. Rapport skills are not considered manipulative if you have positive intent.

Pacing and Leading

Rapport allows you to build a bridge to another person's world. Once pacing is established, you can then begin to lead the other. By definition, pacing and leading is the naturally-occurring human pattern of identifying and utilizing someone's model of the world. Some of the patterns may appear to defy logic, and that's their beauty.

- *Descriptive pacing* is when a manager or trainer acknowledges something that the employee or learner **knows** is true, for example, "You've read this part of the text...", and links this statement to another statement that **might** be true, for instance "...so you're learning how to do these things." If the employee or learner concurs with the first statement, then he or she will be more willing to agree with the second statement. This pattern allows the employee or learner to move from the description of present experience to representation (usually visualization) of another possible or future experience. (See later section on *Milton Model*) Very young children already use this linkage pattern with their parents: "You love me, so buy me this new toy." Or "It's sunny out; let's go to the beach." Even apparently opposite concepts can be linked in this way, for example, "The fact that you have doubts about this article means you're checking out how these ideas will really work." Or, "If you're skeptical about the value of studying history, you owe it to your skepticism to find out more about how it works."

- *Verbal pacing* requires the matching of representational words (visual, auditory, or kinesthetic). For example, if the learner's primary representational system is **kinesthetic**, he or she may say, "I **feel** that I can't get a **grasp** of this subject". The teacher can immediately establish rapport through matching the words by responding, "It seems to me that you want to **get in touch** with the **feeling** of **getting a handle** on this." A **visual** learner might say, "I really can't **see** myself passing this subject." The teacher can say, "**Focus** on your goals so we can **see** where you want to be." Mismatching the representational system will neutralize efforts or diminish existing rapport.

What Specifically Do You Mean?

Whether you are an employer, parent, therapist, student, or instructor, you can, with skillful questioning, clarify misleading or vague utterances and incomplete information. Any sentence can have both a superficial and an abstract composition. The former, the *surface structure*, is what is actually read or heard. The latter, the *deep structure*, contains the true interpretations of the intended meaning. Colloquialisms, a struggle for those learning a new language, often hide accurate meanings. People often limit their own behavior and this is reflected in their speech. Reconnecting the speaker with the deep structure expands perceptions, and generates awareness of expanded choices about how to feel and behave.

The NLP Meta Model is based on the work of family therapist Virginia Satir, and is useful for gathering accurate information. What follows is just a small sampling of patterns.

WARNING: Be cautious with how you use the following models. You can easily upset family members and friends if you get overenthusiastic in your initial practice.

- "I'm angry" can be clarified by asking, "At whom / about what?"

- "They're out to get me" can be understood by asking, "Who specifically are out to get you?"

- "She's smarter" can be narrowed down by asking, "She's smarter than whom — or is she smarter than she used to be?"

- "My boss frustrates me" can be specified by asking, "In what ways does your boss frustrate you?"

- "The decision is made" can be clarified by asking, "Who is deciding what?"

- Words such as: **all, always, everybody,** and **never** are absolutes and often erroneously used for emphasis. If a student says, "I never get anything right," the teacher can respond, "You mean never ever in your whole life?" or, "What specifically do you get wrong?"

- Words such as have to, **should, must,** and **it's neces- sary,** can be challenged by asking, "What would happen if you didn't?" Words like **can't** and **it's impossible** can be challenged by asking, "What stops you from…?"

- Sometimes, people "mind-read." For example, "I know she hates me" can be explored by asking, "What does she do to convince you that she hates you?"

Enticing the Subconscious

Milton Erickson's hypnotic language patterns are on the opposite side of the coin of Satir's focused model. Milton's phrases are purposefully vague, so as to engage the imagination of the subconscious mind by confusing the critical faculty of the conscious mind. His phrases lack meaningful content, thus allowing the client (learner) to adapt a personalized, internal orientation suitable to his or her own model of the world.

- A reference to an obvious indisputable condition sets up an agreement set (known in the sales industry as a 'YES' set), for example, "You are sitting here, listening to me..."

- An illusion of choice such as, "Do you expect the change to take place now or later today?"

- When one thing is implied to cause another, for example, "Since you are attending this class, you are learning the important points of the lesson."

- Assumptions such as, "You realize that you have all the necessary resources."

- Two things or conditions can be equated such as, "You know the answer, so you are an excellent student."

- A vague prompt, such as, "... and notice how easily you begin..."

- Generalizations without referential index, for example, "... so every time you think of that..."

- Rules of possibility or necessity such as, "You can change overnight," or, "You should understand this now."

- Mind-Reading, for example, "I know that you're learning a lot today."

How Simple Words
Can Impact Someone's Life

As children, we trust the wisdom and life experience of our caretakers. The pattern is basically "My ideas = your reality". The teacher-student relationship awakens this pattern with remarkable influence. Once teachers discover that their power of suggestion becomes a self-fulfilling prophecy, they are more vigilant of their speech. A statement like, "Last year's class did miserably on this test, do what you can", can be rephrased as,

"Even though this may seem to be a difficult exam, I know each of you will do better than you think you can, and some of you might even find it a breeze." (See Chapter 9 on *Waking Hypnosis*.)

The Instructor's Turf

Earlier, while discussing the comfort zone, I pointed out that people seek and thrive on predictability. Here is a simple way that instructor can capitalize on that characteristic to enhance the control of their interaction with the learners. In NLP terms, it is called an *anchor*. This elegant, yet simple, idea requires a bit of preparation. The instructor pre-selects a number of precise floor locations to be linked in the learners' minds with specific themes.

For instance, to encourage group participation, the instructor could always stand in the same spot while asking questions. This anchor will always covertly prompt students to contribute when the teacher is in that position. There could also be a locale for fun, as well as one for serious or important information.

Another anchor could be a timeline, with the "past" being to the learners' left, and the "future" to their right. "Now" could be directly in front. As the instructor talks about past challenges, present conditions, and desired outcomes, he or she could either walk the line, or simply gesture. Problems can be flung into the past by simply miming the action. This is helpful for the kinesthetic learners.

Another anchor could be a contingency *trash* spot. This would be reserved for an uncomfortable situation, such as an argument between instructor and learner. Rather than contaminating existing anchors with the negative dynamics and accompanying emotions, the instructor could move to the trash spot while the interaction took place.

A hypnotherapist colleague of mine, Fred Gordon, recalls a teacher from his early schooldays who had a routine of sitting on the edge of his desk at a specific point in the lesson. This informal act signaled the students that he was now ready for dialogue. Fred also remembers that if a student challenged this teacher, he would stand up and move away from the desk. This is a brilliant example of someone who intuitively knew the power of anchors.

If you're an instructor, or just expect to give a presentation sometime, here is an interesting story for you. Remember the consultant in Chapter 5 who identified the red carpet as the source of the class discipline problem? Well, this same consultant also advised that if teachers want to hold the attention of the students, they should wear a small red object like a broach, scarf, or tie. I usually wear a red tie for my presentations. It works like a charm.

> *Good teaching is one–fourth preparation and three–fourths pure theatre.*
>
> Author Gail Godwin

The Learning State

This process is believed to help with whole-brain functioning. (See *Whole-Brain Learning and Hemispheric Dominance* in Chapter 2.)

Developed from both James Braid's 1843 book *Neurypnology* and the practices of the ancient Hawaiian healing art of *Huna*, peripheral vision is used to help a person enter a light trance state. This receptive, focused state is achieved by concentrating for up to two minutes on the spot between one's own eyebrows. Alternatively, as you will read in the next chapter, a focus can be placed on a point behind the skull. While instructing learners to enter this state, instructors will watch for signs of relaxation, such as a slower respiration rate, less facial tension, and dilation of the eyes. Once the state is attained, the learners can then lower their eyes to the instructor or the book to be read. (See reference to "wall-eye" condition of traumatized children in Chapter 5 on *Emotions and Learning,* and Chapter 11 on *PhotoReading*™.)

NLP is taught all over the world in many languages, and has applications for business, education, sales, and therapy. I took my first NLP course in 1993 and it served me well in my corporate career. As a manager, it enhanced my interpersonal skills when dealing with staff, as well as both internal and external clients. On the personal level, I was more aware of the fact that what was said was often not what was meant.

1. **What is your greatest learning from this chapter?**

2. **What is your greatest strength as a person? Think about your job, your family life and your community life as you answer this question.**

3. **CALL TO ACTION:**
    Visit www.UnleashingBook.com to link to the CLI site. Choose the free self-coaching tool entitled "The Brain Walk® – Value Amplification." This tool will invite you to select a value in which you are already strong (for example giving respect, honesty, compassion). Next, the tool will assist you in amplifying that value, giving you the ability to become even stronger in that value.

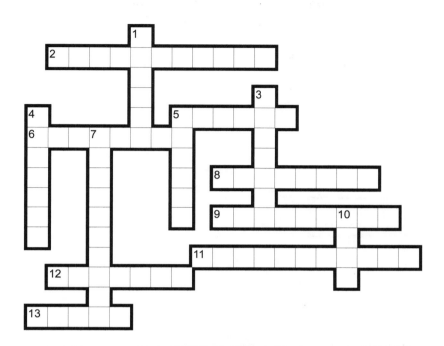

ACROSS

2. Person with the greatest _____ controls the state of affairs

5. _____ learners to speak and read quickly

6. In communication, the _____ validates the message

8. Study showed that the majority of _____ were kinesthetic learners

9. Very precise questioning

11. _____ learners stand close when talking to someone

12. _____ Time people have a good sense of time

13. How someone fits into the society at large: model of the _____

DOWN

1. Purposefully vague phrases: _____ Model

3. A bridge to the other person's world

4. Auditory learners may have difficulty with _____ directions

5. Matching of representational words is _____ pacing

7. The learning state used _____ vision

10. Explicit meaning _____ structure

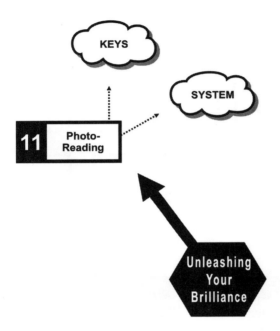

PHOTOREADING

Information for this section has been written with the kind permission and assistance of

Paul R. Scheele, MA
Author of the book *PhotoReading*™

> *Some books are to be tasted,*
> *others to be swallowed,*
> *and some few*
> *to be chewed and digested.*
>
> Francis Bacon

PhotoReading™ **is a uniquely nonconscious activity, not to be confused with speed reading, which is a conscious process. What follows is not meant to be a comprehensive training course of PhotoReading**™**. It is intended to give you an appreciation of how the technique works, and the benefits available once you take a PhotoReading**™ **course.**

As discussed earlier, the school curricula that most of us experience, promote left-brain learning in order to cater to the majority of learners. One striking example of this is how we are taught to read. The left hemisphere is designed for sequencing, language, working with details, and creating internal dialogue. The right hemisphere, suited for handling spatial information, sees the big picture before the details.

The style of reading that we learned in elementary school has condemned us to engage in a somewhat passive activity, without a clear sense of purpose. We usually plow through all types of reading material at the same rate, expecting to comprehend everything at the first pass. We are expected to recognize the structure, grasp the key terms, understand the gist of the events or main argument, remember details, critique the content, and finally be able to quote correctly. That's a tall order. It's no wonder that some learners drop out of school in frustration. Their conscious minds become so inundated that they just "zone out." Learners are taught to strive for comprehension at any cost. This means that in order for them to sequence the information into a logical stream, their reading pace can be painfully and unnecessarily slow.

Keys to More Efficient Reading

The selection theories discussed in Chapter 2 come into play here. The *Early Selection Theory* professed that information had to first pass through conscious awareness in order to be processed for meaning and permanently encoded. Obviously, some educators still believe this to be true. This view was displaced by the *Late Selection Theory* of how data are received and encoded by the nonconscious mind **prior** to being available to the conscious mind. As well, I summarized Professor Rensink's research on nonconscious visual perception. Consciousness is not essential for memory and learning. The essential approach to PhotoReading™ is to trust the power of your nonconscious mind.

As also discussed in Chapter 2, any learning technique that exploits the power of both sides of the brain will produce a synergistic outcome. Paul R. Scheele has built on his knowledge of subliminal perception and preconscious processing by incorporating features of NLP and speed-reading in his development PhotoReading™. This system is based on the fact that the mind can absorb visual information without involving the conscious mind. The right hemisphere will provide the tools to synthesize the material, create internal images, interpret the data, and respond intuitively. The left hemisphere will provide the necessary analysis and sequencing to logically integrate the data. PhotoReading™ facilitates the reading of one page every second with superior recall and comprehension.

In order to master PhotoReading™, you must be prepared to let go of old paradigms. Abandon old habits of procrastination, perfectionism, performance anxiety, and the necessity to know everything right away. The key here is to believe in the power of the intuitive abilities of your nonconscious mind, and trust it for the powerhouse it is. Also, there is no place for low self-esteem or self-doubt.

The Five Steps Of The PhotoReading™ System

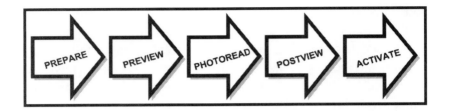

1. Prepare

1.1   To initialize the process, it is vital for you to explicitly state the purpose for reading the specific piece. Your intention may appear to be obvious; however declaration will give energy to the process on both the emotional and physical levels. This strengthening of your objective will engage the mind and increase focus. For example, "I am reading this book to _____ *state your intention*." You can clarify your purpose by posing questions. For instance, ask yourself what you will do with the material covered, the level of detail desired, how much time should be devoted to the reading, and how important the material is for you personally. Do you want the big picture or some specific details? Although simple, this short process is extremely valuable.

1.2   Now enter the *Ideal State*. This physically-relaxed, mentally-alert condition was described in chapter 10 as the accelerated learning state, and is associated with peak human performance. At first, this state is light, and later you will use a slightly deeper one. To reach it, use your peripheral vision, or as Paul Scheele puts it, soft eyes. (See Chapter 5 on *trauma-induced peripheral vision*.) It can also be engaged by focusing attention on a point above and behind your head. The state is similar to viewing one of those novelty 3-D posters. In this flow state, you will be totally absorbed. You will experience a wider visual field, a fluid movement of the eyes, and the ability to read phrases and whole sentences at a glance. In contrast, reading each word (hard focusing) channels the information to your conscious mind. A soft focus, which is not the same as spacing-out or defocusing, allows data to drift into your nonconscious mind, and ultimately the whole brain. Information drawn in through divergent eyes, the periphery of the visual field, is processed non-consciously. At this juncture in the process, it is **not** necessary to consciously understand the content.

2. Preview

2.1   The initial step in Preview involves surveying the material, while in the Ideal State. You do this by scanning the titles and subtitles, the text on the back cover, the table of contents, and any text in bold print or in boxes and charts. Terms unique to the subject will stand out. This part should take only a minute. It supports the long-term memory and builds a mental structure by categorizing and classifying the data that will soon follow.

2.2   Now it is decision time. Assess what you've done in your Preview phase, and decide if you will continue to the next step in the process, or abandon this particular book because it does not meet your stated intention.

3. PhotoRead

This is sometimes called the "flip-flip" phase. To set the optimum climate for the process, assume a playful and open attitude. Don't expect to remember any of this material consciously. That's not the point. There are eight parts to this step.

3.1   *Prepare:* Gather the reading material. State your intention and expectations. Assume a good posture.

3.2 Enter a *resource level* with a few deep breaths. This will shift your body and mind into a relaxed state. It turns on the right hemisphere, preparing it for input.

3.3 At this point, you can energize your intention by using some of the tapping tools described in chapter 8.

3.4 Since negative thoughts inhibit learning, make some affirmations in order to stimulate the absorption of material. For example, "I desire the information in this ____ book title ____ to accomplish my purpose of ____ restate purpose ____."

3.5 For the actual PhotoReading™, a slightly deeper state is required. This is called the *PhotoFocus* state. This soft gaze allows you notice the whole page at once.

3.6 The conscious mind attempts to interfere with the process by putting up perceptual defenses. These can give you tunnel-vision, thereby sabotaging the process. To maintain the steady state, you must distract the conscious mind. You can do this through deep rhythmic breathing, combined with an audible chanting in time with the page turning. For instance, "re-lax, re-lax, one — two — three — four." With feet on the floor and legs uncrossed, position the reading material so that its surface is 90 percent to the line of sight. Flip the pages at the rate of one page-turn per second or two. It doesn't matter if some pages are missed. The information is spontaneously processed by the nonconscious mind.

3.7 When you finish PhotoReading,™ give the following affirmation, "I acknowledge all feelings evoked by this experience." You may then add, "I am curious as to how many ways my mind and body can demonstrate that this information is available to me," or, "I release this information for my body and mind to process."

3.8   Now, visualize or imagine the information flowing from the right brain to the left. This is now the time to just let the mind begin its integration process.

4. Postview

4.1   After the PhotoReading™ step, spend five minutes to think about the important items.

4.2   You can re-stimulate your neural connections by being active and purposeful. Identify and make a list of trigger words. Students can review exams from previous years. This activity will generate a curiosity and strengthen a desire to learn more.

4.3   Generate questions for later review. You can begin with, "What is important to me in this book?" The purpose here is to encourage an inquiring mind. This should take about seven minutes.

5. Activate

5.1   An important component in this process is an incubation period of at least twenty minutes, and ideally overnight.

5.2   Following this interlude, in a state of relaxed alertness, review all the questions that you prepared earlier. Another method to activate is to discuss these core concepts with others. This will clarify your ideas and feelings about the material.

5.3   The next activity builds on what has been done so far, and involves the intuition in a radar-like pursuit. It is called the *super read and dip*. Here, you allow your nonconscious mind to guide you to specific sections of the text that attract you. With your gaze open, hunches will draw you to certain titles and subheadings. The signals to dip and explore do not involve the conscious mind. Just as in the PhotoReading™ itself, ignore thoughts that pages were missed. What are being appraised are not words, but meaning bits, such as phrases, thoughts, feelings, and ideas. If you have prepared specific questions, the information will leap out at you during this exercise.

> A tip that will help you here is to skim over the upper-half of the letters of a sentence. To test how effective this is, use a sheet of paper to cover the top half of the letters and notice that it's difficult to read. Then cover the bottom half and see how easy it is.

5.4   Rather than digging for details, the point of everything so far is for you to understand the gist of the author's train of thought. This mental summary incorporates the main argument, the problem, and the solution. By categorizing the material, you perceive its structure.

5.5   *Skittering* is an effective alternative for those who are analytical. Based on the belief that only four to eleven percent of text carries meaning, the brain captures key words, while feeling secure that missed ones are unimportant. Here are the steps:

- Enter the Ideal State and review your purpose

- Read the title, subtitle, preface and the first few paragraphs

- Choose a paragraph. Read the first sentence. Move your eyes all over the paragraph in many different patterns. Your brain will pick up key words. Read the last sentence, then go to a new paragraph and repeat this process.

- Read completely the last few paragraphs and the summary.

- Review and reflect.

5.6   Now create a *concept map* as described in Chapter 1. This will synthesize the material.

5.7   *Rapid Reading* is done if you feel that you need more information after completing the other four steps. Before you begin, ask yourself what you specifically want more of. Once you decide that you need more, begin reading from the beginning of the book. Rapid Read speeds are highly flexible. Flash through the book, slowing down only at words or phrases that you recognize, or seems to address your purpose.

Astrid Whiting is a Medical Exercise Specialist in Victoria, Canada. The certification exam of the American Academy of Health, Fitness and Rehabilitation Professionals demands a mark of 100 percent on all case studies. For the many study hours that Astrid spent preparing for the exams, she used the PhotoReading™ techniques without doing this final step (Rapid Read). She achieved the required 100 percent. By the way, this was also the first time she had used the PhotoReading™ system. Need I say more?

PhotoReading™ Skill-building

Like many of the processes covered in this book, I just want to whet your appetite so that you can explore books and courses that will take you to a new level. See this book's web site for a link to this resource.

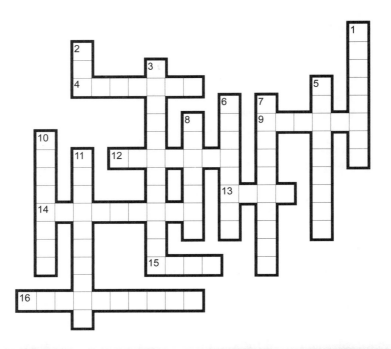

ACROSS

4. To initialize the photo-reading process, state the _____

9. Postview re–stimulates the _____ connections

12. One of the last steps is to create a _____ map

13. _____ selection theory: data are received and encoded by the nonconscious mind first

14. The key is to believe in the power of _____ abilities

15. Photofocus state displays a _____ gaze

16. Step of 20 minutes following post-viewing

DOWN

1. Other name for photoread step

2. Photoreading incorporates features from _____

3. Photoreading is an _____ activity

5. To master photoreading let go of old _____

6. Theideal State is physically–relaxed, _____–alert

7. "Skittering" is an effective alternative for those who are _____

8. Examining the titles and subtitles and book cover, and table of contents

10. Rapid Read speeds are highly_____

11. A soft gaze

BRILLIANT NOTES

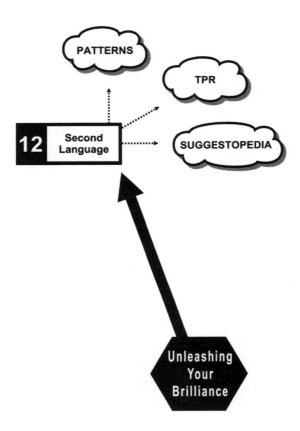

12

SECOND LANGUAGE LEARNING METHODS

Language Learning Patterns

> *We don't learn to have arms rather than wings. Why, then, should we suppose that our brains acquire their fundamental structure through learning rather than genetic inheritance?*
>
> Noam Chomsky

The human brain evolved over millions of years to have a genetically-determined adaptation for language. Known as *innate knowledge*, it is inherited through the structure of the brain. By analyzing how infants learn language, we can further our understanding of how our brain works. We can then apply this knowledge to learn anything more effectively.

In infancy, children are proficient, dynamic negotiators of their own conceptual expansion. In a child's first two years, there is a repetitive exchange of language-body signals between caretaker and infant. Infants as young as three months old can imitate vowel sounds. Studies have shown that newborns mimic the mouth movements of vowel and consonant sounds they hear from adult models, even when they cannot see the adult's mouth moving.[46] Because of body movements, most babies internalize an intricate *linguistic map* of how the language works prior to initiating understandable speech.

The wiring of the brain enables language acquisition in a linear progression with comprehension first, then production. Talk cannot and will not be generated until the infant has internalized sufficient details in the linguistic map. Early on, a child learns an incredible ten words a day. Young children achieve comprehension **before** they speak. Research has shown that this linear progression from comprehension to production is often over 90 percent successful in reaching fluency in a second language. When production is forced on students before they understand, the success rate drops to a meager 4 percent success rate.

From the third grade through to university, school systems have routinely, and almost exclusively, catered to the left side of the brain. Classrooms are designed in rows and columns to facilitate serial delivery in written and oral form. Not all students can integrate input aimed solely at the left half of their brain.

Dr. James Asher, developer of *Total Physical Response* (TPR), claimed that second language learning should be based on the model of first language learning. The model has three vital aspects: understanding the spoken language must come before speaking, understanding is developed through body movement, and the listening period creates a readiness to speak. This model teaches that speaking should never be forced.[47] When the adult's internal linguistic map is imprinted with enough detail of a new language, talk is spontaneously released in a similar manner to that of infants. As with the infant, speech is distorted, fragmented, and develops in slow-motion compared with the flashing speed that the student has been internalizing the comprehension.

Total Physical Response (TPR)

Infants acquire language using an unconscious process where they deduce patterns of what they hear. This *mental grammar*, which in actuality is a set of language rules, allows them to understand and eventually construct new words and sentences. The process is initiated by the caretaker through a rich interaction of language-body "conversations" that continue 16 hours a day throughout the formative years. The adult speaks, and the infant answers with a physical response such as turning the head, smiling, crying, reaching, grasping, and walking.

The first achievement in language acquisition, known as comprehension literacy, is the exquisite skill of understanding the target language. Internalizing and understanding the *phonology* (sounds), *morphology* (word changes), and *semantics* (meaning) of a target language is not a minor achievement. It cannot be rushed. Eventually, when children have encoded their linguistic map and decoded enough of the input, they reproduce the language quite spontaneously.

Learning from Babes

An ideal teaching method would duplicate first language acquisition by using whole-brain learning and employing activities related to social interaction. It would stimulate phonological processing involving the production of speech sounds, the relationships between these sounds, and the development of word order and creative language. Based on how a first language is acquired, an American psychology professor, James Asher, developed this innovative technique for teaching a second language.

Total Physical Response (TPR) was introduced in the 1960s, and is based on the premise that language is best acquired when the learner receives lots of understandable input. This is linked to physical actions that are designed to reinforce comprehension. Understanding the spoken language must precede speaking. As with infants, the linguistic map is being constructed without any demands to talk. Premature speaking may minimize rapid vocabulary development, likely cause anxiety, reducing the "stickiness" of the words being learned, and could harm long-term pronunciation if bad habits are collected before hearing a sufficient amount of language.

Understanding of the parents' commands is developed through body movements. The listening, or silent period, produces a readiness to speak by unconsciously or implicitly forming the grammatical rules. Once the neural circuits are in place, speech is spontaneous. This is known as *delayed production* (See *Baby-Signing* later in this chapter). This requires an intricate transmission of data between both sides of the brain. Body movement stimulates data flow from left to right and back again at lightning velocity. Dr. Asher has called this *brain-switching*. Any instructional strategy that has this feature should be successful with most students for first trial learning, long-term retention, and zero stress. That is exactly what TPR offers.

The channels of learning engage all senses: sight, hearing, taste, touch, smell, speaking, and all motor activities. Each individual finds learning easiest through one or some combination of these channels. TPR is considered *brain compatible*, and so this means that short and long-term retention is maximized. Workplace vocational courses and military forces have always made use of TPR principles.

The typical school environment, however, confines and restricts the student both physically and emotionally. The left-brain instruction combined with minimal body movement in the limited territory around the student's desk and chair has a dampening effect on mental processes. With TPR, space expands rather than contracts. Students are in motion, using their bodies to respond to directions in the target language. As with all other accelerated learning techniques, TPR engages the student through a supportive and fun classroom environment.

A typical TPR activity might contain instructions such as "Stand-up, walk to the window, open the window, return to your seat, sit down." Students internalize the target language rapidly in huge chunks rather than word-by-word. Initially the students simply watch, then later actually perform the actions. All of this happens with the understanding that they are not expected to speak, at least until they are ready. Such activities can be both fun and motivating. After a fairly limited amount of repetition, the learners, even without verbalization, assimilate the actions and words. The interaction among students can continue for hours after the TPR class is over. Students can play with the target language using utterances to direct each other. In the movie *Lilies of the Fields*, Sidney Poitier uses TPR to teach English to a group of German nuns.

TPR allows students to achieve comprehension and fluency considerably faster than infants because infants are limited in their range of physical responses. By comparison, school children and adults enjoy an enormous range of physical movements such as writing, cooking, drawing pictures, driving vehicles, playing games, operating computers, riding bicycles, and so on.

Pre-verbally, infants express their needs through gestures. Most babies, eager to communicate at eight or nine months, soon realize that signing will get them what they want. Observations of deaf parents signing with their "hearing" babies have revealed that, since these babies could express their thoughts and needs more easily, they were less demanding. A growing form of parent–infant communication is **Baby–Signing**. No prior knowledge of sign language is required, and infants can be taught to sign as young as six to eight months. Research shows that Baby–Signing builds linguistic and literacy skills, reduces frustration, enhances self–confidence, and lays a solid linguistic foundation that lasts a lifetime.

TPR Advantages

- It involves both left and right-brained learning.
- Rapid understanding of the target language.
- Long-term retention lasting weeks, months, even years.
- Simple to understand, yet does require skillful application to be effective.
- Significant positive transfer from listening to reading and writing skills.
- Zero stress for both students and the instructor. It lowers the affective filter.
- Academic aptitude is a negligible factor.

- Works for most languages including sign language, mathematics, and science.

- Suitable for all levels of second language instruction.

- Drop-out rate can be reduced.

- Good for kinesthetic learners who need to be active in the class.

- Suitable for large or small classes.

- Excellent for mixed-ability classes.

- Very effective with teenagers and young learners.

TPR Challenges

- Teaching abstract vocabulary and expressions requires extra effort and preparation. For example, the instructor can use vocabulary cards on which abstract words are written. For teaching the abstract word "bright," the teacher could ask the students to "Pick up the bright card and bring it to me." The students would comply and check the meaning of bright in the dictionary afterwards.

- Some students may find it embarrassing and refuse to participate. By forming students into teams, their anxiety would be reduced.

- Lesson plans must be well thought out.

- TPR also demands patience and flexibility in case the students cannot follow the commands in the correct way.

- It is difficult for even the most skilled and inventive teacher to prolong a class involving directions and physical responses for more than a few minutes before the activity becomes repetitious. Situational role-play could provide a wider range of contexts.

- TPR is not a complete method. It cannot do the entire job

of language teaching, nor was it designed to do this. It must be interspersed with other techniques before boredom and adaptation sets in.

TPR Technique

Typically, the instructor will invite a couple of students to sit up front and listen carefully to what is uttered in the target language (with no translation) and do exactly what they see the instructor doing. Asher's research suggests that most of the grammatical structures and hundreds of vocabulary words can be learned through an instructor's skillful use of imperatives. The instructor then says in the target language, "Stand," and stands up gesturing for the students to rise. Then, "Sit," and everyone sits down. Elaborations follow, such as, "Stand, Walk, Stop, Turn," etc. After hearing the directions a number of times and acting along with the students, the instructor sits down and invites individual students to perform alone in response to the instructions. The intent is to make obvious to the students that they have indeed internalized the unfamiliar words and understand them correctly. The process of understanding through the body continues, and at some point, each student will be ready to talk.

Although most will be prepared to talk within ten or twenty hours, a few will be ready almost immediately. It is important to respect each student's readiness to talk. Pressure to speak at this point will backfire. When students begin to talk, it will not be perfect. There will be many distortions, but steadily, pronunciation will improve. As mentioned earlier, those learning after reaching puberty will usually have an accent.

As the process continues, the student internalizes more and more details about the phonology, morphology and semantic structure of the target language. The linguistic map imprints at a rapid rate with an ease that gives the illusion that nothing is happening. After about ten or twenty hours of TPR instruction, the instructor invites those students who are ready to assume the role of the instructor and utter instructions to guide the behavior of fellow students and the instructor.

TPR and Grammar

TPR lessons should be immediately followed by standard school grammar. With TPR at the core, the grammar portion comprises about 30 percent of the whole lesson. Beyond the imperatives and present tense, TPR is easily extended to other verb tenses and more complicated sentence patterns by using gestures and props. Teachers are able to add enough non-linguistic context to their speech to convey meaning to the learners.

TPR Conclusion

The student dropout rate in a traditional second language program can be as high as 95 percent. Studies at the University of Texas and elsewhere show that this stunning attrition rate can be reversed when TPR is a central feature of the language program. The reason that TPR dramatically reduces attrition is that it is a model confidence-builder since, in a very short time frame, the student realizes substantial improvement.

Suggestopedia

The appropriate use of suggestion results in an enormous increase in an individual's ability to remember new material, and to integrate it into the personality. In the 1970s, Bulgarian psychologist Dr. Georgi Lozanov designed a technique of eliminating negative suggestion from, and introducing positive suggestion into, the learning process. *Suggestopedia* was based on elements of hypnosis, yoga, and Soviet psychological research on extra-sensory perception. It fixes material into the subconscious using music during "concert" sessions. Lozanov discovered that the brain has an almost infinite potential for learning if the subconscious mind receives information in the right way.

His work was greeted with great cynicism. To validate his theories he founded a language school in his native Bulgaria. He proved that Suggestopedia could deliver a 300 percent improvement in the speed and effectiveness of learning. Years later, his technique migrated to the west, where it was registered as *Superlearning*® in the USA.

In order to speak a language, one must be able to hear it correctly. Native languages encode or program people to hear in different sound frequency ranges. For instance, the French hear within a range of 800 – 1,800 Hz., the British 2,000 – 12,000 Hz., the Italians 2,000 – 4,000 Hz, and the Americans 750 – 3,000 Hz. The subtleties of French vowels are jammed into a narrow band and may simply be undetectable to those whose ears are not "tuned-in."

To compound this reality for language learners, many experience age-related hearing loss. Sound therapy music has proven beneficial in extending auditory range. In addition to this predetermined condition, a person's attitudes and limiting beliefs hamper learning.

Dr. Lozanov noticed that as we get older, we tend to accept prevailing social norms and adjust our personalities to be conventional – to fit in. We acquire self-limiting beliefs about learning. We often sacrifice our learning opportunities in order to conform to these outside limits. Our childhood capabilities are set aside, and no longer used. They are preserved, however, as functional reserves. According to Lozanov, these functional reserves can be reintegrated into the active personality through the use of suggestion. (See Chapter 9 on *Hypnosis.*)

The primary use of positive suggestion is to transform limiting beliefs and habits. Two of the major difficulties in language learning are memorization and integration. This technique uses Baroque music and relaxation to induce a light trance, increase concentration, and strengthen absorption of the material. Movement and activities, which allow learners to integrate the content into their personalities, are also incorporated. (See Chapter 4 on *Kinesthetic Intelligence,* and Chapter 8.)

The Method

The original Suggestopedia program incorporated NLP techniques, such as presuppositions and anchoring, along with waking hypnosis suggestions. New students were subjected to a screening process, and just being accepted into the program convinced them that they were special. The class would begin with all students changing their names. This new identity encouraged new behaviors and aspirations, and often released shyness. The method produced dramatic results in short order, thereby bolstering the students' confidence.

Over the decades since the original method was introduced, it has evolved into a number of variations. The core components are the teacher's enthusiasm, a positive classroom environment, and the music.

Baroque largo (slow) movements help the student to reach a certain state of relaxation, in which the receptivity is increased. Some of the composers from the Baroque period are Bach, Handel, Pachelbel, and Vivaldi. Voices and solo instruments standing out against the orchestra are likely to distract the student. Ideally, the orchestra should have the same instruments played throughout the work. The best choice is string orchestras. Research by Lozanov has shown that, even without suggestion, when Baroque music is used during memorization, it can improve recall by at least 25 percent.

A Typical Session

1. A fun upbeat piece of music to welcome the students is followed by a three-minute relaxation period using a Baroque largo music piece (60 beats per minute).

2. New material is presented. Usually read in a normal fashion by the teacher.

3. A twenty-minute *active concert*. The teacher reads the subject text in an animated fashion with lots of dramatic gestures. The dynamics of the music is matched by varying voice level and pitch to complement the movement of the music. In order to form an image or structure of the content and context, the students just listen. They can follow along in their text, underlining, highlighting, or making notes as they wish. Although the students have a translation of the text at this stage, it is collected after the concert session. They will work without it for the remainder of the course.

4. Another active concert approach is to have the students repeat phrases after the teacher. This is done in time with the music. If vocabulary flashcards are used, one side contains an English word with its counterpart in the foreign language on the reverse. A strict breathing pattern is employed: two seconds: breathe in / four seconds: utter words on each side of the card / two seconds: breathe out. To make each flashcard more impressive, the speaker should use different intonations and rhythms. The three commonly-used intonations are *loud/commanding*, *soft/confidential*, and *normal*. Individuals have the option of tape-recording their own session for later play-

back. A typical twenty-minute session would use about 150 flashcards.

5. A three-minute state-breaker using a faster (allegro) baroque movement (120 beats per minute) brings the students back from their light trance. Standing up, stretching, and deep breathing can also be used here.

6. A twenty-minute passive concert, in which the students close their eyes and listen to the teacher, who reads more or less normally to the accompaniment of slower baroque music. This is followed by a break state activity.

7. An activation process is required to facilitate integration into the students' personalities. This allows them to manipulate and play with the language. It may include activities consisting of acting out portions of the text, singing specially prepared songs, playing games, telling stories, carrying on short conversations, and performing psycho-dramas. This phase occupies approximately 75 percent of the time, and is followed by another break state activity.

Two additional steps can be taken to enhance the integration of the material. The practice sessions can be recorded for later playback. The music acts as an anchor of the words and phrases. The other integration technique is future-pacing. Here, learners can imagine fluently speaking the new language at some time in the near future. They can picture a conversation in a business, social, or familiar scene.

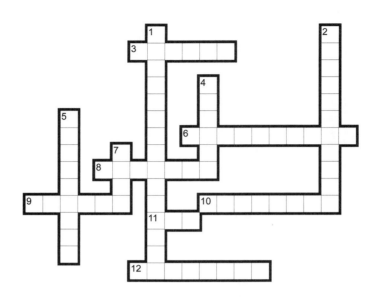

3. Practice sessions can be recorded for later play-back. The music acts as an _____ of the words and phrases

6. Word changes

8. Bach, Handel, Pachelbel, and Vivaldi are composers from the _____ period

9. During the _____ concert, the teacher reads the subject text in an animated fashion with lots of dramatic gestures

10. Dr. Lozanov said that as we age, we acquire self-_____ beliefs about learning

11. Suggestopedia was partially based on elements of Soviet psychological research on _____

12. Pre–verbally, infants express their needs through_____

1. The human brain's geneti-cally–determined adaptation for language

2. A growing form of parent/infant communications

4. Young children achieve comprehension _____ they speak

5. The meaning of words

7. The original Suggestopedic program began with each student changing his/her _____

BRILLIANT NOTES

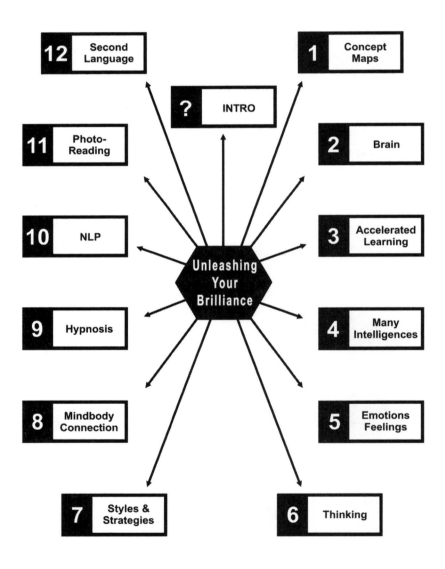

13

SOME FINAL WORDS

> *To know one's strengths,*
> *to know how to improve them,*
> *and to know what one cannot do*
> *are the keys to continuous learning.*
>
> Peter F. Drucker

Have you heard the story of the man who went into a book store and asked the clerk where the Self-Help section was? The clerk replied, "If I told you, then that would defeat the whole purpose, wouldn't it?"

I've heard that 25 percent of people who purchase self-help products never even open the packages. Clearly, you're not part of that group. After attending self-help events, most people are motivated to transform their lives. They are excited about all the positive changes that are about to take place. Regrettably, for most of them, there will be no lasting changes in behavior, no enduring transformations, and no long-term achievement. Their initial enthusiasm fades within days. Why does this happen? What is the missing ingredient for the 90 percent who have wasted their money? What they have failed to create is an **action plan**.

Now that you have completed this book, you are in an excellent position to begin your plan. Begin by determining what outcome you want. For example, you might desire better grades, a promotion, greater understanding of some subject… whatever. Just write down the things that you want to accomplish and why. The reasons you state will not only validate your plan, they will furnish some extra motivation. The ultimate goal will then have to be subdivided into realistic chunks. If you need help here, reread the section on *goal-setting* in Chapter 3.

Throughout this book, my central theme has been that each of us learns in a unique way. What works for me doesn't necessarily work for you. You may have to defend your own rights against indifferent managers or instructors, or inflexible institutions. Blaming others for your challenges is a cop-out. It doesn't advance your cause. If the way you learn is not being supported, be proactive… be assertive… **Take control of your learning and be all you can be**.

Let me conclude this book with words from Mark Twain:

Twenty years from now you will be more
disappointed by the things that you didn't do
than by the ones you did do.

So throw off the bowlines.
Sail away from the safe harbor.
Catch the trade winds in your sails.

Explore. Dream. Discover.

APPENDIX 1 GLOSSARY

ADD	Attention Deficit Disorder occurs in people who have a malfunction in the sensory input areas of the brain. Stimuli are apparently not filtered properly and consequently they cannot focus well.
ADHD	Attention Deficit Disorder With Hyperactivity. In a 1981 study, insufficient amounts of essential fatty acids were discovered in a large number of hyperactive children. Since boys have a three times higher need for essential fatty acids than girls, this might explain why a larger number of boys than girls have some problems in various areas of learning and behavior.
Associative	The ability to perceive relationships, connections, links, and comparisons.
Attachment Disorder	A condition where individuals have difficulty to form loving, lasting, intimate relationships. It can originate anytime between conception and the age of two years through deficient bonding, unwanted pregnancy, abuse, unsettled or inconsistent parenting, birth trauma, or the intake of toxins by the expectant mother.
Baroque music	Music composed from 1600 to 1750.
BRAC	Basic Rest/Activity Cycle: An ultradian rhythm of brainwaves with a duration of 90 to 120 minutes.
Brainstorming	A creative process where a diverse group of people contribute random and spontaneous ideas in order to solve a problem. One or two people write the ideas on a whiteboard or flipchart as they are generated. No other commentary or critique is permitted. Ideas on the board may trigger additional thoughts. Participants must be willing to be silly and playful thus allowing greater creativity.
Deductive	Considering the big picture first, this "top-down" approach works from the more general to the more specific.

Developmental Readiness	This is a sign that a child's brain is "ready" to do the hard thinking necessary to learn left-hemispheric subjects. Usually between five to seven years of age.
Dysgraphia	A short-circuit between the brain and the hand, exhibited when letters are formed with great stress, high pencil pressure, and inconsistent shape and/or placement on the line.
Dyslexia	A reading disorder characterized by an inability to interpret spatial relationships or to integrate visual and auditory signals.
Essential Fatty Acids	The Omega 6 oils are found in salad dressing, mayonnaise, and safflower and sunflower oil. Omega 3 fatty acids are found naturally in fish, flaxseed oil, wheat germ, and nuts and seeds. Navy beans and oatmeal also provide some essential fatty acids.
Flow State	An optimal learning condition typified by high challenge and low stress.
fMRI	Functional Magnetic Resonance Imaging: A brain scan technique.
Gustatory	The sense of taste.
Hippocampus	This part of the brain is associated with the formation of memory. It is linked directly with all senses and the limbic system.
Ideographic	An adjective used to describe the communication of an idea through pictures, symbols, and icons. In some written languages (like Chinese), the symbols represent ideas or objects, rather than sounds.
Idiot Savant	A person with autism possessing a single exceptionally well-developed skill or talent in spite of cognitive deficiencies in most other areas. The single skills are usually musical or mathematical. It is more common in males by a factor of six to one.
Inductive	Beginning with the specific observations and measures, this "bottom-up" approach reveals patterns that can be studied in order to develop general conclusions.

Initial Sensitizing Event	Root cause of a problem, often a long-past specific event.
Limbic System	The part of the brain housing the emotions.
Mid-brain	Known as the early mammalian brain, it includes the limbic system where the emotions reside.
Mind-body	A term designed to highlight the true link between the mind and body.
Moro Reflex	A startle reflex established in the embryo.
NASA	National Aeronautics Space Agency of the United States of America.
Neocortex	The "thinking brain." Essential in language, problem-solving, forward planning, fine movement, and creativity.
Neurocognitive	The study of how the brain changes during the process of learning.
Neurogenesis	The ability for brain cells are able to rebuild themselves after having been destroyed by surgery or trauma.
Neurons	Nerve cells that make up the nervous system.
Neuroscientist	One who studies the nervous system.
Neurotransmitter	Chemical messengers that carry information within the brain.
NLP	Neurolinguistic Programming.
Numerate	To have a keen ability to work with numbers.
Olfactory	The sense of smell.
Onomatopoeia	The formation or use of words that imitate their referent. e.g. boom, hiss.
Parasympathetic Nervous System	That part of the autonomic nervous system that acts to slow down or otherwise mitigate the excitement of the fight-or-flight response, also known as fight/flight/freeze.
Parietal Lobes	That part of the brain that identifies incoming sensory information.

PET	A brain scan technique, Positron Emission Tomography employs a small amount of radioactively-tagged glucose in order to reveal activity areas of the brain during specific cognitive or physical activities.
Phonemes	A minimal unit of speech sound.
Presuppositions	In NLP, beliefs and expectations that give us greater choice and allow us more freedom.
Proprioceptors	Sensory nerve endings in muscles, tendons, and inner ears that provide information about body position and balance.
Psychometrics	Measurement of mental traits, abilities, and processes.
RAS	Reticular Activating System: Part of the limbic system, it is responsible for learning and memory among other things.
Reptilian Brain	The oldest part of the brain, it is an expansion of the upper brain-stem, located at the top of the spine. It is responsible for survival.
Sympathetic Nervous System	That part of the autonomic nervous system that is sometimes called the fight-or-flight system. When activated, it begins to shut down the detoxification and digestive systems.
Syntax	Rules governing the formation of grammatically-correct phrases and sentences.
Temporal Lobes	The part of the brain associated with hearing and memory. The conduit between the thinking brain and the emotional brain (limbic system).
Transactional Analysis	Developed in the 1950s by Dr. Eric Berne, and popularized by Dr. Thomas A. Harris in his book *I'm OK — You're OK*. Three distinct ego states coexist in each person. These three states determine how we act and interact. They are called the *Parent*, the *Child*, and the *Adult*.
Triune Brain	The three-part brain: Reptilian, Limbic System, and the Neocortex.
Vestibular System	Responsible for posture, equilibrium, and maintenance of visual plain as head changes attitude, and eye-gaze directionality.

APPENDIX 2 NON-INTERNET RESOURCES

Amen, Daniel G. (1998) Change Your Brain, Change Your Life.
Tomes Books: New York

Armstrong, Thomas PhD (1999) 7 Kinds of Smart.
New American Library (Penguin): New York

Brooks, Michael (1989) Instant Rapport. Warner Books Inc.: New York

Budzynski, TH (1976) Biofeedback and the Twilight States of
Consciousness. Plenum Press: New York

Buzan, Tony (1993) The Mind Map Book. BBC Books: London

Covey, Stephen R. (1989) The 7 Habits of Highly Successful People.
Fireside: New York

Dennison, Paul (1992) Brain Gym®.
Educational Kinesiology Foundation

Grinder, Michael (1989) Righting the Educational Conveyor Belt.
Metamorphous Press: Portland OR

Hannaford, Carla PhD (1995) Smart Moves.
Great River Books: Salt Lake City, UT

Maclean, Paul (1990) The Triune Bzrain in Evolution.
Plenum Press: USA

Meier, Dave (2000) The Accelerated Learning Handbook.
McGraw-Hill: New York NY

Ostrander, Sheila; Schroeder, Lynn (1997) Super-Learning 2000.
Dell Publishing: New York

Pert, Candice (1997 & 1999) Molecules of Emotions.
Simon & Schuster: USA

Restak, Richard (1984) The Brain. Bantam Books: New York

Restak, Richard (2001) Mozart's Brain and the Fighter Pilot.
Harmony Books: New York NY

Stokes, Gordon, Whiteside (1984) One Brain: Dyslexic Learning
Correction and Brain Integration. Burbank CA

Weil, Andrew MD (1995) Spontaneous Healing.
Alfred A. Knopf Inc: New York

Wenger, Win PhD, Scheele, Paul R. (2002) Genius Code:
Learning Strategies Corporation: Minnetonka MN

APPENDIX 3   SYMPTOMS THAT MAY BE HELPED BY THE FEINGOLD PROGRAM

*The following symptoms are not to be considered abnormal —
many people exhibit some of them at times.*

*A person who may be helped by the Feingold Program
displays more of them more frequently
and to more of an extreme than the average person.*

Behavior

- **Marked Hyperactivity**

  Constant motion, running instead of walking, inability to sit still,
  inappropriate wiggling of legs / hands

- **Impulsive Actions**

  Disruptive behavior / disturbs others, unresponsiveness to
  discipline, poor self-control, destructive behaviors: throws, breaks
  things, little or no recognition of danger to self, unpredictable
  behavior, inappropriate noises, excessive and/or loud talking,
  interrupts often, abusive behavior to people or pets

- **Compulsive Actions**

  Perseveration (repeating an activity)

  Touching things / people, aggression, workaholic habits, chewing
  on clothing, other objects, scratching, biting, picking at skin

Emotional Concerns

- Low frustration tolerance, oversensitive to touch, pain, sound,
  lights, depression, frequent crying, demands immediate attention,
  irritability, panics easily, nervousness, low self-esteem, mood
  swings, suicidal thoughts

Learning / Developmental

- **Short Attention Span**

  Impatience, distraction, failure to complete projects, inability to listen to whole story, inability to follow directions

- **Neuro-Muscular Involvement**

  Accident prone, poor muscle coordination, poor eye-hand coordination, difficulty writing and drawing, dyslexia / reading problems, speech difficulties / delays, difficulty with playground activities, sports, eye-muscle disorder (nystagmus, trabismus) tics, some types of seizures.

- **Cognitive & Perceptual Disturbances**

  Auditory processing problems, visual processing problems, difficulty in comprehension and short-term memory, disturbance in spatial orientation (up-down; right-left), difficulties in reasoning (math problems and word meaning)

Health / Physical Complaints

- **Poor Sleep Habits**

  Resistance to going to bed, difficulty falling asleep, restless / erratic sleep, nightmares, bad dreams

- **Frequent Physical Complaints**

  Ear infections, asthma, leg aches, bed wetting, stomachaches, constipation, daytime wetting, headaches, diarrhea, hives or rashes, congestion

APPENDIX 4 SOLUTIONS

Finished Files

In the introduction, you read a short passage, and were asked to count the number of times that the letter "F" occurred. Most folks find only three or four. Actually there are six. If you didn't count the "F" in the three occurrences of the word "OF", it is because you are mentally pronouncing that word "OV." What an interesting mind we have!

Crossword Puzzle Solutions

Introduction

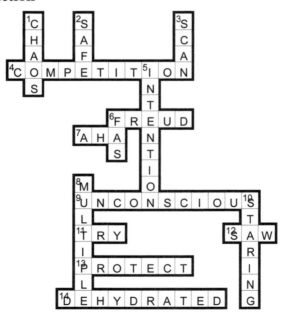

Chapter 1

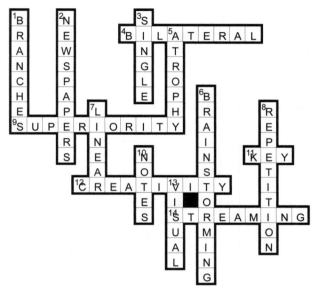

Chapter 2

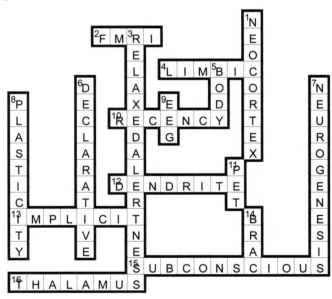

Chapter 3

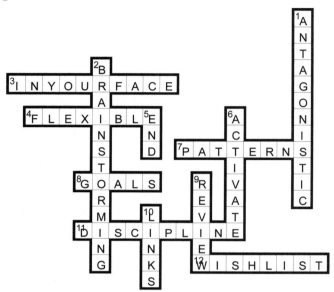

Chapter 4

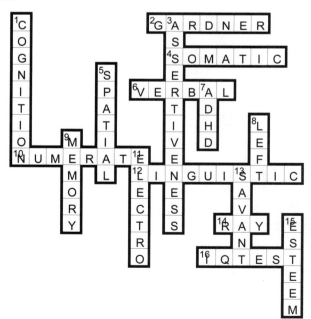

Chapter 5

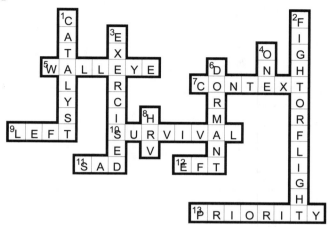

Chapter 6

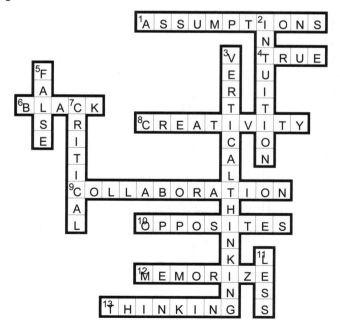

Chapter 7

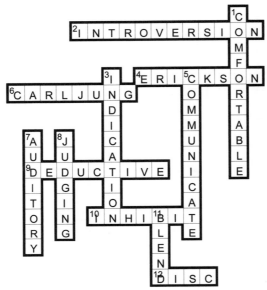

Chapter 8

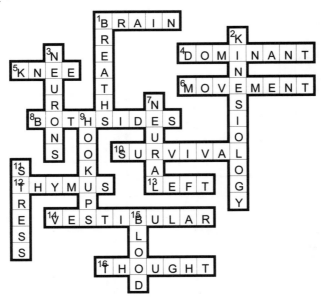

Chapter 9

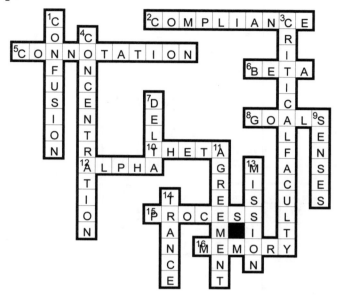

Chapter 10

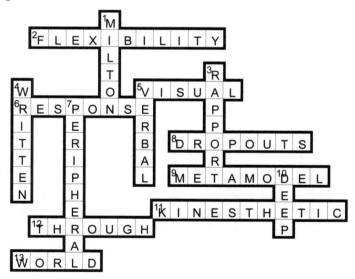

Chapter 11

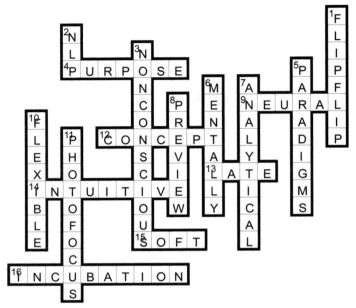

Chapter 12

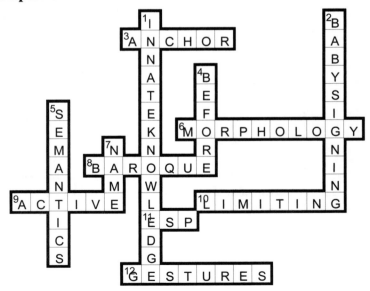

APPENDIX 5
RANDOM WORD ASSOCIATION BRAINSTORMING

Telephone Company Example

The telephone company formed a group of employees who were to focus on the issue of how to increase revenue from their pay phones. The process has four simple steps.

1. The group is asked to nominate a random word. Common nouns work well. In the absence of nomination from the group, a dictionary is a useful source (of, say, the first common noun on a page opened at random by a group member).

    For the telephone company's exercise, the random word was 'pipe'. The facilitator wrote this word on the center of a flip chart.

2. Each member of the group is asked for one word that he or she associates with the random word on the flip chart. These associated words are written on the flip chart page around the random word in the center.

    The words associated with the random word 'pipe' by the telephone company group were: lead, bag, water, and smoke.

3. The facilitator now asks the group to focus on the issue/purpose of the exercise, i.e. to find a solution to the problem. The group is then asked to select a word from the page, and brainstorm solutions related to the word.

    In this case, the group brainstormed solutions related to the associated words of bag, water, lead and smoke. They were asked: "How does bag (or water or lead or smoke) relate to increasing revenue from pay phones?"

4.   The brain then has to find a fit for two seemingly dissimilar concepts. All ideas are recorded, and group members are encouraged to build on each other's ideas. As with all brainstorming techniques, all ideas are considered equally valuable. It is often not the first idea that is the best solution, but one that builds on a previous idea.

For the phone company exercise, the best idea came from the word 'lead'. The idea was to make the phone handsets very heavy so that people would get tired of holding them, and thus limit the length of their phone calls. This idea was implemented, and revenue increased by 35 percent in one year.

Appendix 6 Reasons For Unclarity

Physical reasons for unclarity:

1.   Amalgams (metal tooth fillings) that generate heavy metal toxicity in the body.

2.   Candida, commonly known as "yeast", produces methyl alcohol to numb our thinking.

3.   Stimulants like caffeine, alcohol, nicotine and other recreational and prescription drugs.

4.   Hypoglycemia.

5.   Hormone imbalance (estrogen, progesterone). Imbalance of the thyroid hormone.

6.   Adrenal glands are working inefficiently.

7.   Poor diet.

8.   Excessive meat/eggs in diet. The fat in meat creates a lining of mucous on the bowel walls which prevents nutrients from entering the bloodstream.

9.   Incomplete digestion, disturbed bowel ecology. Poor absorption of vitamins & minerals.

10.   Essential Fatty Acid deficiencies, therefore, inability to secrete neurotransmitters.

11.   Too little fat in the diet (high risk of suicide).

12.   Parasites.

13.   Severe pain.

14.   Constricted receptors in the body prevent nourishment from reaching our thinking cells.

Intellectual reasons for unclarity:

1. No desire to change old habits.

2. Inability to accept new ideas.

3. Lack of understanding of how multiple intelligences bring us the greatest wisdom.

The emotional and spiritual reasons for unclarity are fewer in number; however they may give us the most grief.

Emotional/Spiritual reasons for unclarity:

1. Disconnection from higher power.

2. Lack of faith in self and others.

3. Poor self-confidence.

4. Depression.

5. Stress.

© Coaching and Leadership International Inc.

ENDNOTES

1   Hannaford, Carla PhD (1995) Smart Moves. Great River Books: Salt Lake City, UT

2   Stansfeld, Stephen (2005) Queen Mary's School of Medicine and Dentistry as reported in The Lancet.

3   Psychological Science (Vol. 13, No. 5, Sept. 2002).

4   Picard, Michel (2004) Université de Montréal

5   http://www.feingold.org/blue-pg.html June 2005

6   Buzan, Tony (1993) The Mind Map Book. BBC Books: London

7   Ostrander, Sheila; Schroeder, Lynn (1997) Super-Learning 2000. Dell Publishing: New York

8   Vingerhoets, Guy; Berckmoes, Celine; Stroobant, Nathalie. "Cerebral Hemodynamics During Discrimination of Prosodic and Semantic Emotion in Speech Studied by Transcranial Doppler Ultrasonography", Ghent University; "Neuropsychology", Vol. 17, No. 1

9   Wellcome Trust UK (2003) as released at the Royal Society

10 Armstrong, Thomas PhD (1999) 7 Kinds of Smart. New American Library (Penguin): New York

11 Peterson, Bret PhD The Evolution of Language - Found on the internet (Feb. 14, brainconnection.com/topics/?main=fa/ evolution-language2

12 Faculty of 1000: evaluations for Rolls ET et al Eur J Neurosci 2003 Aug 18 (3):695–703 http://www.f1000biology.com/article/12911766/evaluation

13 Meier, Dave (2000) The Accelerated Learning Handbook. McGraw-Hill: New York NY

14 Amen, Daniel G. (1998) Change Your Brain, Change Your Life. Tomes Books: New York NY

15 Kennedy, B., Ziegler, M.G., and Shanna-off-Khalsa, (1986) Alternating Lateralization of Plasma Catecholimines and Nasal Patency in Humans. Life Science

16 Wenger, Win PhD, Scheele, Paul R. (2002) Genius Code: Learning Strategies Corporation: Minnetonka MN

17 http://www.rense.com/general48/mappingthesixthsense.htm
    & CBC Interview February, 2004

18 Wenger, Win PhD, Scheele, Paul R. (2002) Genius Code:
    Learning Strategies Corporation: Minnetonka MN

19 Neimark, Jill (1995) "It's Magical, It's Malleable. It's...
    Memory." Psychology Today

20 0040405.wstartzero0405/BNStory/specialScienceandHealth
    (April 5, 2004)

21 http://www.new-oceans.co.uk/new/education/accel.htm
    March, 2004

22 Witelson SF, Glezer II, Kigar DL (1995). Women have greater
    numerical density of neurons in posterior temporal cortex.
    Journal of Neuroscience 15:3418–3428.

23 Cahill, Larry (2005) - His Brain, Her Brain. Scientific
    American April 5, 2005

24 McCraty, Rollin PhD; Barrios-Choplin, Bob PhD, Atkinson,
    Mike; Tomasino, Dana B.A. (1998) The Effects of Different
    Types of Music on Mood, Tension, and Mental Clarity:
    Alternative Therapies in Health and Medicine

25 Maclean, Paul (1990) The Triune Brain in Evolution.
    Plenum Press: USA

26 Pert, Candice (1997 & 1999) Molecules of Emotions.
    Simon & Schuster: USA

27 Covey, Stephen R. (1989) The 7 Habits of Highly Successful
    People. Fireside: New York

28 Meier, Dave (2000) The Accelerated Learning Handbook.
    McGraw Hill: New York NY

29 http://heartmath.org/education/testedge/cd.php Aug.20/04

30 http://seattlepi.nwsource.com/health/180524_condor05.html
    July 5, 2004

31 Oxford, RL & Lavine, RZ (1992) Teacher-Student Style Wars
    In The Language Classroom. ADFL Bulletin 23(2)

32 Middleton, Frank A., Strick, Peter L (1994) Anatomical
    Evidence for Cerebellar and Basal Ganglia Involvement in
    Higher Cognitive Function.

33   Hannaford, Carla PhD (1995) Smart Moves.
     Great River Books: Salt Lake City, UT

34   Restak, Richard (2001) Mozart's Brain and the Fighter Pilot.
     Harmony Books: New York NY

35   Restak, Richard (1984) The Brain.
     Bantam Books: New York

36   Stokes, Gordon, Whiteside (1984) One Brain: Dyslexic
     Learning Correction and Brain Integration. Burbank CA

37   Brain Gym® is a registered trademark of the Educational
     Kinesiology Foundation.

38   Weil, Andrew MD (1995) Spontaneous Healing. Alfred A.
     Knopf Inc: New York NY

39   www.LifeWave.com

40   Ward, Byron J. PhD; Howell, Deborah PhD(c) (2004) Using
     Hypnosis to Enhance Learning in General Psychology
     Classes. Journal of Hypnotism, March 2004: National Guild
     of Hypnotists

41   Budzynski, TH (1976) Biofeedback and the Twilight States of
     Consciousness. Plenum Press: New York

42   Argyle, M. (1970) British Journal of Social and Clinical
     Psychology, volume 9

43   Perry, Michelle (2005) – Associate Professor of Educational
     Psychology, University of Illinois

44   Grinder, Michael (1989) Righting the Educational Conveyor
     Belt. Metamorphous Press: Portland OR

45   Brooks, Michael (1989) Instant Rapport. Warner Books Inc.:
     New York NY

46   Faculty of 1000: evaluations for Chen X et al Dev Sci 2004
     7 :42–47 www.f1000biology.com/article/nonpub18596/
     evaluation

47   Romo, Theresa (Summer Institute 2001) – Found on
     the internet (Feb. 10, 2004) du/Web percent20Journals/
     articles2001/TROMO_~1.HTM

BRILLIANT NOTES

INDEX

A

B

C

READERS' COMMENTS...

"Although traditional education is often brain-antagonistic, this book offers dozens of helpful strategies to make learning brain-compatible and shows how to take your learning to the next level of effectiveness."

Paul R. Scheele, Chairman, Learning Strategies Corporation
Author, PhotoReading and Natural Brilliance

"As a college lecturer, already familiar with NLP and hypnosis, I was particularly interested in what else was out there in the accelerated learning field. Wow... this book sure opened my eyes. I now have a number of new tools in the old toolbox."

Dave Hallett CH, MH, CI
Director, Canadian Hypnosis Centre

"Excellent for those responsible for learning in an organization."

Robert W. Swaim, Ph.D.,
Director, Peter Drucker Executive Development Program - China

"Brian's extensive research and precise style of writing has given me access to information that would have taken me years to discover on my own. This is a great learner-friendly book that I am excited to share with my friends and colleagues."

Gizelle S. River,
TeleLeader Trainer and Business Coach

"This should be required reading for any student of any age, and anyone wanting to rise to higher levels of performance."

Roy L. Streit, Certified Hypnotherapist,
NLP & EFT Master Practitioner

"This assembly of techniques from diverse sources have been masterfully combined in this book enabling me to become instantly more productive with new learning skills and habits. The quantum leap in my learning and comprehension abilities from the use of just one suggestion was worth the price of the book."

Owen Rose, Town Planning Consultant

"I have personally used many of the strategies outlined in this book to accelerate not only my own results, but the results of those I train on a day to day basis."

Astrid Whiting, Medical Exercise Specialist,
Nationally-Certified Personal Trainer

"Brian's book is an operations handbook and self-directed guide so we can successfully navigate the growing sea of information and ideas we are forced to live in. Thanks Brian, it's a lifesaver!"

Linda Schaumleffel,
Facilitator of "Cutting Edge Fitness for Your Brain"